ASPECTS OF HUDDERSFIELD

ASPECTS *of* HUDDERSFIELD

Discovering Local History

Edited by

Isobel Schofield

Series Editor
Brian Elliott

Wharncliffe Publishing Limited

First Published in 1999 by
Wharncliffe Publishing Limited
an imprint of
Pen and Sword Books Limited,
47 Church Street, Barnsley,
South Yorkshire. S70 2AS

Copyright © Wharncliffe Publishing Limited 1999

For up-to-date information on other titles produced under the Wharncliffe imprint, please telephone or write to:

Wharncliffe Publishing Limited
FREEPOST
47 Church Street
Barnsley
South Yorkshire S70 2BR
Telephone (24 hours): 01226 - 734555

ISBN: 1-871647-66-5

A CIP catalogue record of this book is available from the British Library

Cover illustration: Huddersfield Market Place. *Kirklees Cultural Service*

Printed in Great Britain by
Redwood Books, Trowbridge, Wiltshire

CONTENTS

INTRODUCTION

by Isobel Schofield

This is the first volume of what is intended to be an on-going series of Local History books about Huddersfield and the surrounding villages. These books are one way of recording the many different aspects of research that is taking place in the town in such a way that this research is easily and interestingly available to everyone.

There is a wide range of subjects covered in this book. From life in the village of Honley as seen through the eyes of the Manorial Court Records that have been transcribed by John Goodchild, to the coming of modern communications with the building of the Moorside Edge Radio Station recorded by John White who worked on the site for many years.

John Rumsby's interesting article describes the earliest coins through to the Co-op milk and bus tokens, the prize medals, miners' and wage checks, many of which may be seen in the Tolson Museum. Alan Brooke has written about the political unrest of the mid-nineteenth century as Chartists campaigned for workers' rights. His chapter includes a recently discovered letter written in October 1838 by Feargus O'Connor to Lawrence Pitkethly.

Oral History is a very important way of recording what has happened to make a village or area unique. The Colne Valley is just one area that has a rich heritage of such legends detailed by John Oldham. A living heritage that is still remembered today in the annual Marsden Moonraking Festival.

Huddersfield's textile heritage is not forgotton with Fred Wood's memories of life in the mills in the 1920s as a young boy. These are illustrated by a selection of photographs that were taken in 1902 in the Stewart and Kaye Limited, Broadfield Mills, at Longroyed Bridge, Huddersfield.

Music is one of Huddersfield's most important contributions to the culture of the town. The Choral Society's reputation is international. One of the first members of the Choral Society was Mrs Susan Sunderland in whose memory a competition is held annually. This biography of Mrs Sunderland includes a rarely published photograph of the first Concert Party from which the Society developed.

Robert Bruce was called to serve as minister at Highfield Congregational Church in 1853. During the next fifty years of his ministry there were many changes in the town – political and educational. The Highfield congregation included the first Mayor of Huddersfield, Town Councillors and Aldermen who were members of the church who also served as Deacons and in the large Sunday School.

The chance discovery of two diaries bring to life a young man's life and courtship in 1923 and 1924. Who he was do not know, but his life makes fascinating reading as he records his work and leisure activities day by day.

I would like to express my thanks to all the authors who have contributed to this book; also the people based at Huddersfield Library who have given of their time and knowledge, especially to the staff of West Yorkshire Archives, Kirklees, the Huddersfield Local Studies Library and the Digital Image Project. A large number of the photographs are taken from the Kirklees Photographic Archive, which includes a wide range of photographs including the *Huddersfield Examiner* Collection. Grateful thanks to Kirklees Cultural Services and the *Huddersfield Examiner* for permission to use these images to bring to life the town's past.

My thanks also must go to Brian Elliott, Series Editor and to Mike Parsons of Wharncliffe Publishing, without whose support and encouragement I would not have been prepared to undertake this work.

Anyone interested in making a contribution to Aspects of Huddersfield 2 should in the first instance, contact Mrs Isobel Schofield Editor, c/o Wharncliffe Books, 47 Church Street, Barnsley S70 2AS, enclosing a brief description of the proposed work.

1. Coins, Tokens and Medals of the Huddersfield District

by John H Rumsby

Coins and other round objects

THE COINS THAT WE SPEND in shops today are in fact 'tokens'. They do not contain their face value of precious metal, but are accepted everywhere as a convenient method of exchange, ultimately backed up by the government's gold reserves. Before the twentieth century the situation was different. A shilling, issued by the government with Royal authority, contained a shilling's worth of silver; a sovereign a pound's worth of gold. Copper coins were also issued by the government, but with less regularity, and so 'small change' was often in short supply, making everyday monetary transactions difficult for humble folk. Therefore 'token' coins were issued by local shop owners and industries and these can often illuminate aspects of local industry. Similarly, numerous other coin-like objects such as co-op checks, work checks, metal tickets and commemorative and prize medals can throw light on the lives of ordinary people. Many of these objects find their way into local museums, and the following study is based largely on specimens in the Kirklees Community History Service collection held at the Tolson Memorial Museum, Huddersfield supplemented by information from local collectors.

The Rich Man in his Castle

The earliest coins that the inhabitants of this area would have seen in any numbers were Roman coins. The local British tribe, the Brigantes, did not use coinage, although their neighbours to the south, the Corieltauvi (or Coritani) had a well-developed currency. That the Brigantes were interested in coins at least as bullion metal is illustrated by a collection of objects found at Honley by workmen in 1893. It consisted of five silver coins of the Corieltauvi, twelve well-worn silver coins of the Roman Republic, six silver and copper-alloy coins of the early Emperors Nero and Vespasian, and some Roman brooches and other trinkets.[1] The coins are typical of the currency in use at the time of the Roman advance into the Pennines in about AD 70-71. It is tempting to interpret the hoard as loot from a Brigantian raiding party; the coins would have been melted down and refashioned into jewellery.

In fact Roman coins are an unusual find in the Huddersfield area, compared with other parts of the north such as eastern Yorkshire. There were no towns or rich villa estates in this agriculturally poor area, and the only fort was at Slack, occupied for only 60 to 80 years. Most trade probably continued to be done on a barter basis. A few single finds of coins represent chance losses, but some hoards have been discovered. Hoards are collections of coins hidden by their owner, often in dangerous times, which were never recovered. One such hoard, originally consisting of about 500 copper-alloy coins, was found near Thurstonland in 1838. Sixty-five of these coins survived to enter the Tolson Museum collection. The latest coins are of Carausius (reigned AD 287-293), and the hoard was probably buried during the troubles associated with this usurper's attempt to separate the province of Britannia from the rest of the Empire. A similar third century hoard was found in the eighteenth century at Thirstin, near Honley.

No coins of the Anglo-Saxon or Viking periods have been reported from Huddersfield. Place-names and sculpture testify to settlements of this period, but coin use must have remained low, perhaps being reserved for paying taxes, whilst barter continued to be used for local transactions. A few medieval coins have been found, including an interesting collection of six silver pennies and one halfpenny of Henry III (1216-1272), found on top of Pule Hill near Marsden. These coins were all of the same type, and were presumably buried at the same time, for safekeeping. They would represent about a day's wages for an artisan.

A more valuable hoard, obviously hidden by a wealthier person, was found in Spring Wood in Netherton in 1892, and is now displayed at the Tolson Museum. It contained 75 English, one Scottish and four Irish coins, and was hidden in around 1645-1646, the date of the latest coins. It is typical of hoards concealed all over the country during uncertain times of the Civil War; for example the much larger hoard from Elland. It is interesting to speculate on the fate of the owner, possibly an officer in the Royalist or Parliamentarian army, who did not survive to reclaim his secret fortune. The types of coin show the profile of official currency in circulation at the time. All were silver, and they included not only coins of the Stuart kings James I and Charles I, but also 33 well-worn coins of Elizabeth I and even a groat (fourpenny piece) of Mary Tudor.

Much of the wealth in rural areas like Huddersfield was locked up in land ownership, and from the sixteenth century some landlords were accumulating large estates by their own shrewd management and business skills, and by judicious marriages. The Ramsdens started to build up their estates in Huddersfield from the 1530s, and their fortunes were closely tied with those of the town until the Corporation 'bought itself' by purchasing the Ramsden lands in the 1920s. Local street names such as Ramsden Street and John William Street still testify to the former glories of this family. There is also an unusual medal, still quite common in the area. This carries the arms and motto of the Ramsdens, and commemorates the coming of age (twenty-one at that time) of Sir John William Ramsden (1831-1914) in 1852 (Figure 1.2-3). No doubt his tenants found it politic to keep examples of the medal on prominent display in the cottages.[2]

One metallic check nicely illustrates the traditional relationship between landowner and tenant. This bears the inscription 'EARL OF DARTMOUTH'S RENT AUDIT' with the value '3D'. (Figure 1.7) These were given to the tenants of the large estates owned by the Earl of Dartmouth, and could be exchanged for refreshment in the local public houses. This replaced the earlier practice of providing a meal for tenants during the annual rent collection.[3] Although the Dartmouth's seat was at Woodsome Hall, the audit took place at Slaithwaite.

Landowners and clergy were usually prominent in other parts of the establishment such as the magistracy. The Tolson Museum contains a handsome bronze Magistrate's Ticket of Admission, which was issued to the Reverend N Holmes, although this gentleman has not been traced. A rather later, but still Victorian, admission ticket was issued by the Huddersfield Country Court. (Figure 1.6) Several tickets or membership passes are also known for local Freemasons' lodges, such as the Huddersfield Truth Lodge No. 521. (Figure 2.8) Freemasonry was much less secretive in the nineteenth century than at the present day, and processions in Huddersfield would include prosperous landowners, businessmen and mill owners proudly wearing their full Masonic regalia.

The pinnacle of the establishment was of course the Royal family. A visit by a 'Royal' was much rarer in the nineteenth century than in these days of limousines and helicopters, and towns often celebrated the honour with a special medal. The first such medal in Huddersfield was struck to commemorate the visit of the Duke and Duchess of Albany in 1883 to open Huddersfield's first public park (Figure 2.5). Beaumont Park was established on land given by Henry Frederick Beaumont, and 600 medals were distributed to school children to celebrate the day. Slaithwaite too had its royal day and a medal was issued to commemorate the visit of King George V and Queen Mary

Figure 1:

1. Marksmanship medal won by Josiah Jenkinson of the Huddersfield Volunteer Infantry in 1812.

2-3. Obverse and reverse of the medal commemorating the coming of age of Sir John William Ramsden in 1852.

4-5. Medal given to the children of Huddersfield to celebrate the peace treaty of 1919 which finally ended the First World War.

6. Magistrate's ticket for Huddersfield County Court.

7. Threepence check given to tenants at the Earl of Dartmouth's rent audit.

All items illustrated are from the collections of Kirklees Community History Service on 11 July 1912 (Figure 2.6-7). Undoubtedly the most important royal occasion of the late nineteenth century was the sixtieth Jubilee of Queen Victoria's reign in 1897. As in towns across the country, Huddersfield indulged in elaborate ceremonies, including processions, church service and, eventually, the erection of the Victoria Tower on Castle Hill.[4] A superior bronze medal was produced by the Corporation for distribution to important personages, and a white metal alloy version was given to schoolchildren. (Figure 2.1-2)

Several local medals refer to national or international events; perhaps inevitably these were mainly wars in which Britain engaged. In 1812 Josiah Jenkinson was awarded a handsome silver medal (Figure 1.1) for being 'Best Shot at Ball Practice'. The medal is engraved with a picture of a rifleman of Jenkinson's regiment, the 3rd (Huddersfield) West Riding Local Militia. (Figure 1.1) The members of this regiment were all volunteers, forerunners of the Home Guard, although the invasion they vowed to repel would have been by Napoleon's French army, not Hitler's Germans.[5] A later generation of part-time soldiers, the 6th Huddersfield Rifle Volunteers also competed for marksmanship prizes, and the medal won by John Thomas of No. 1 Company in 1861 is also in the Tolson Museum.[6] These rifle volunteers were again formed to repel a perceived threat from France, but after various convolutions of title and function were eventually transformed into the Territorial Army, giving vital service in two wars. Huddersfield commemorated the first of those world wars by presenting its children in July 1919 with a special peace medal, bearing a design of a figure of Victory surrounded by a soldier, a sailor and an airship. (Figure 1.4-5)

Health Spiritual and Temporal
In today's secular society it is difficult for us to realise how important religion was in the lives of the majority of people in earlier times, especially the nineteenth century. The various churches, Anglican and non-conformist, provided not only spiritual rules to live by, but also a full social life, and often through its church and Sunday schools a source of education otherwise denied working class children until the *1870 Education Act*. The influence could be all pervading. A pious mill owner would expect to see his workers in church or chapel on a Sunday if they were to keep their jobs secure.

The occasion that provoked the issue of perhaps more commemorative medals than any other was the centenary in 1880 of the foundation of the Sunday school movement by Robert Raikes. Many thousands of medals, in a number of varieties, were distributed

Figure 2:

1-2. Medal issued by the County Borough of Huddersfield to commemorate Queen Victoria's Diamond Jubilee in 1897.

3-4. Obverse and reverse of the medal issued in Huddersfield to celebrate the coronation of King Edward VII in 1902.

5. Medal commemorating the opening of Beaumont Park in 1883 by the Duke and Duchess of Albany.

6. Medal commemorating the visit to Slaithwaite of King George V and Queen Mary in 1912.

7. Medal commemorating the visit to Marsden of King George V and Queen Mary, on the same day as their visit to Slaithwaite.

8. Ticket for the Huddersfield Truth Freemasons' Lodge No. 521.

to Sunday schoolchildren, and they form a frequent enquiry in museums. The most common variety shows a portrait of Robert Raikes on one side, on the other a scene of Christ surrounded by children with the appropriate text from St Mark's Gospel (10.14) 'Jesus said suffer the little children to come unto me and forbid them not for of such is the Kingdom of God'. These medals were localised by the addition of a clasp fastened to the top, (Figure 3.2) on which was engraved the name of the church or chapel, such as Ramsden Street Independent, Buxton Road Wesleyan or Paddock New Connection. St Paul's Church issued its own medal in 1907 to commemorate a new school building. (Figure 4.6) The inscriptions reads:

> *In the faith of the Lord Jesus Christ these schools were built to continue the work of religious and secular education as conducted in the old schools in Princess St. Huddersfield from AD 1846 to AD 1906.*

Another medal celebrating buildings works was the 1887 medal (Figure 3.3) marking the restoration of Kirkheaton Parish church after a disastrous fire. This medal doubles as commemoration of Queen Victoria's fiftieth Jubilee of the same year. Pole Moor Baptist Church similarly issued medals marking the 1897 Jubilee and the Coronation of King Edward VII in 1902. (Figure 3.1)

Physical health is commemorated more rarely than spiritual well-being. Surprisingly there is no medal marking the opening of the Huddersfield Infirmary in 1829, although the Tolson Museum does have a fine enamelled Award of Merit given to Mrs Avis Elizabeth Butler in 1942 for her nursing service. An early attempt at provision of facilities for disabled people was the Cripples' Guild founded by the Reverend W Heap at the Queen Street Mission, now the Laurence Batley Theatre, in 1907 (note the influence of the church). A 'Cripples' Home' was established at Lindley Moor, donated by John Sykes, and a medal of 1928 celebrates the twenty-first anniversary of the Guild. The home closed in 1939, although the Guild continued.

Education
As has been said, churches and chapels played an important role in elementary education in the early Victorian period. However, there was also a secular movement, the Mechanics' Institution (or Institute), which illustrates the saying 'Tall oaks from little acorns grow'. Huddersfield and its satellite villages supported a number of these institutions, which provided libraries, lectures and study facilities for the 'artisan classes' seeking to better themselves by further education. The Huddersfield Institution, whose origins date

Figure 3: 1. Medal issued by Pole Moor Baptist Chapel to celebrate the Royal Jubilee of 1897. **2.** Medal commemorating the centenary of the Sunday School movement, given to children of Ramsden Street Independent Chapel in 1880. **3.** Medal commemorating the Royal Jubilee of 1887, and the restoration of Kirkheaton Parish Church in the same year.
4. Trade token issued in 1666 by George Dixon in Honley and Holmfirth.
5. Trade token issued in 1668 by Nicholas Greaves of Almondbury.
6. Trade token issued in 1666 by Edmund Walker of Huddersfield.
7. Trade token issued in 1670 by John Dyson of Slaithwaite.
8. Trade token issued in 1792 by John Downing, tea dealer and grocer of Huddersfield.

back to 1825, went through several transformations, occupying the still-surviving building in Northumberland Street from 1861 to 1884, before moving to the stylish new Technical School, opened in 1883. This school formed the nucleus which grew into the Polytechnic and more recently became Huddersfield University.[7] The opening of the School was marked by a Fine Art and Industrial Exhibition, opened on 7 July 1883 by the Duke of Somerset, whose daughter had married Sir John William Ramsden. The catalogue of the exhibition demonstrates the wide range of products manufactured in the town at the height of its industrial prosperity.[8] A medal commemorating the opening bears a fine representation of the new School, as well as the crest of the Ramsden family. (Figure 4.5) A variant couples the Technical School obverse with that of the medal for the opening of Beaumont Park in the same year, with the portrait of the Duke of Albany. Thus purchasers could have two souvenirs for the price of one!

In contrast to the working-class self-help of the Mechanics' Institutions was the public school, represented in the numismatic record by the splendid prize medals of the Huddersfield College.[9] The college was opened in 1839, and premises were constructed in the then-fashionable Tudor style in New North Road. This building still survives as an annexe of the University. The prospectus of the College declares its aims to be that of

> *providing for the youth of the middle and upper classes a sound Classical, Mathematical and Commercial Education, upon a Scriptural foundation.*[10]

The presentation of various gold and silver medals was commenced in 1841 and continued until the 1870s. All the subjects taught were represented: English Composition, History and English Declamation, Classics, Mathematics, Commerce, French and German. Amongst the prize winners were many who became prominent citizens. For example, the Carlisle Medal (English Essay) for 1872, now in the Tolson Museum, was awarded to D F E Sykes who later practised as a solicitor in Huddersfield, and wrote a still valuable history of the town. William Henry Broadbent (Mathematics 1849), the son of a small manufacturer at Longwood, became physician to Queen Victoria and King Edward VII and was rewarded with a baronetcy. Other prize winners became church ministers, teachers, doctors and in one case Bishop of Trinidad. Less fortunate was Henry de Paiva, winner of the Morpeth Medal in 1842, who reportedly died of overstudy whilst a student at Cambridge!

King James's Grammar School in Almondbury, originating in the

Figure 4:
1. Huddersfield College Prize Medal for German awarded to A Midgley in 1867.
2. Huddersfield College Commercial Medal awarded to John Foster in 1851.
3. Advertising check for Sykes and Abbott's patent educational machine in 1881.
4-5. Commemorative medal for the opening of the Huddersfield Technical School and Mechanics' Institution in 1883.
6. Medal commemorating the rebuilding of St Paul's Church Schools in 1907.

sixteenth century, also awarded prize medals, of which the most prestigious was the Dartmouth Medal, first presented in 1854 by the 5th Earl of Dartmouth. The Dartmouth Medal continued to be awarded annually until 1969, after which it was replaced by the King James's Medal.[11]

An advertising check reminds us of a piece of private enterprise in education, at a time when many companies and individuals were competing for the supply of furnishings and educational gadgets to the new Board Schools set up after the 1870 Act. The check was issued in penny, halfpenny and farthing size, by Ezra Sykes and Otho Giles Abbott. The obverse shows the Queen's head, and the reverse a seated schoolboy operating Sykes and Abbott's device for teaching spelling and arithmetic. (Figure 4.3) The patent (12 November 1881) describes this as a series of discs on shafts equipped with tablets bearing letters, numbers etc. which could be rotated. Abbott was Clerk to the Huddersfield School Board, so there may have been a conflict of interest if he tried to sell it to local Board Schools!

The World of Work

Although Huddersfield is best known for its textile production, the area in fact supported a wide variety of industries, many of which are represented in the numismatic record. The district was once rich in coal, one small relic of which is the lamp check. (Figure 6.67) These are usually made of copper alloy or white metal, circular, pierced near the rim, and bear the name of the colliery company or pit, and a stamped number. Each miner was issued with two of these checks, stamped with his own work number. When he collected his lamp he left one check on the hook, and handed in the other on going underground. In the event of an accident, it was easy to see by the checks left at the surface which men were still underground.

Figure 5. Huddersfield College in 1839, from a print prepared by the architect, J P Pritchett of York. *Kirklees Cultural Services*

Figure 6:

1. Wage check of Messrs Lockwood and Keighley, Upperhead textile mills, Huddersfield.
2. Work check of Huddersfield Corporation Tramways.
3. Wage check of W and E Crowther, textile manufacturers of Slaithwaite.
4. Wage check of Central Mills, Huddersfield.
5. One hundredweight check of the Huddersfield Gas Company, dated 1854.
6. Lamp check of Lepton Edge Colliery.
7. Lamp check of the Old Silkstone Colliery Company.
8-9. Medal commemorating the one millionth motor manufactured by Brook Motors of Lockwood in 1950.

Although no working pits are left around Huddersfield, these checks testify to the many collieries that once existed both before and after nationalisation, such as Denby Grange, Lepton Edge and Emley Moor. [12] (Figure 6.6-7)

One of the dependant industries of coal-mining was the gas industry, which itself gave rise to the chemical and dyeing industries which are still among the biggest employers in the town. A check marked 'Huddersfield Gas Company 1854' with the weight of $\frac{1}{2}$ CWT (hundredweight) is thought to have been for the sale of coke, a by-product of the gas process (Figure 6.5). Payment would be made at a cash office, and the customer issued with this check for exchange in the yard for coke.

The most common type of work check, usually although not exclusively associated with the textile industry, is the wage check. (Figure 6.1-4) These are usually of copper alloy, with the company's name around the edge, and a number stamped in the centre. Each employee had his or her own number, corresponding to a wage list, and would be issued with a check. Wages were normally brought round the mill (thus saving time lost from workers queuing at the wage office), the money being contained in small metal cups each marked with the appropriate worker's number. The cups were often placed in wooden trays resembling school inkwell trays. Each worker collected his or her wage from the cup, and handed in the check as a receipt. The Tolson Museum collection contains many of these wage checks, (Figure 6.1) such as the octagonal check of Lockwood and Keighley of Upperhead Mills, Huddersfield, manufacturers of Bedford Cords, Velveteens and other fancy cloths, and that of William Child of Shelley, who made imitation seal-skins and Astrakhans. The museum also contains the checks, (Figure 6.3) wage pots and trays of William and Elon Crowther, a Slaithwaite firm originating in the late nineteenth century, and still in operation. In 1918 they advertised 'fancy woollen cloths...including Cheviots, Saxonies, Coverts, Mantle, Dress, Overcoating and Showerproof cloths made at Crimble and Brook Mills'.

By the 1850s Huddersfield textiles had already established the reputation for high quality that they still hold. Many prize medals were awarded to local firms, such as the Bronze Medal given for samples exhibited at the Great Exhibition of 1862 by Day and Watkinson of Railway Street, woollen manufacturers and merchants, (Figure 7.2) or the 'Fourth Award' given at the International Exhibition at Sydney, Australia in 1879 to W Hicks, teazle merchant (and also 'manufacturer of the self-fastening button'). [13] Local awards include the First Prize silver medal given in 1884 by the Yorkshire Union of Mechanics'

1

2

Figure 7:
1. Bronze Medal from the Great Exhibition in London, 1851, awarded to J
W and H Shaw in Class XII (Woollens).
2. Bronze Medal from the International Exhibition in London, 1862,
awarded to Day and Watkinson, woollen manufacturers and merchants of
Railway Street, Huddersfield.

Institutions to James Crosland, woollen manufacturer of Paddock for his cloth designs. (Figure 8.1)

Other industries represented by medals illustrate those such as engineering that grew up originally to service the textile mills but later established independence and a nation-wide reputation. For example, Brook Motors of Lockwood started in business making electrical motors for powering textile machinery. In 1950 they issued a medal commemorating their one-millionth motor. (Figure 6.8-9) The descendant of this company is still in operation. Rippon Brothers by contrast originated as a carriage-maker in the middle of the nineteenth century, but adapted very successfully in the early 1900s to the new business of motor-car bodies, making bodies for luxury cars such as Rolls Royce. In the 1930s the Institute of British Carriage and Automobile Manufacturers awarded them several silver medals for coachwork exhibited at the Olympia exhibitions held in London. (Figure 8.5)

The need to provide skilled workers for industry is no recent phenomenon, and the Huddersfield Engineers Training Association was formed in 1916, when wartime conditions, including the introduction of conscription, must have made the supply of industrial labour an anxious task. The Association offered gold, silver and bronze medals to students the gold being awarded to 'the most brilliant all round student in any year of his Diploma course.'[14] (Figure 8.3)

Getting to Work: Transport
Today Huddersfield streets are choked with private cars, but up until the 1950s most journeys were still made by public transport. Railways were much used for local trips before the Beeching cuts of 1965 closed many small stations such as Holmfirth. Horse-drawn buses, and especially trams, trolleybuses and motorbuses were the main transport method for getting to work and also for leisure activities.

Some public houses owed their existence, or at least their names and much of their customs to the transport system and issued their own checks or tokens (see below for the use of these). (Figure 10.1,4) These issuers included Berry Brow's *Railway Hotel*, and both the *Traveller's Inn* and the *Railway Hotel* in Honley. A previous method of transport, the canal system is recalled by a twopenny check of the *Fly Boat Hotel* in Huddersfield.

The most common local transport checks, however, are those issued by Huddersfield Corporation for use on its own public transport network. (Figure 6.2) There are a wide variety of these, mostly made from various colours of plastic, although some are of copper alloy or white metal. The first tokens were issued in 1896 to postmen who used trams to travel to their postal rounds. These

Figure 8:
1. Cloth Workers First Prize Medal of the Yorkshire Union of Mechanics'
Institutions awarded to James Crosland of Huddersfield in 1884 for designs
in cloth.
2. Bronze Medal presented to W Willans for services to the Great Exhibition
of 1851.
3. Student's Silver Prize Medal of the Huddersfield Engineers Training
Association, 1917.
4. Gold Medal of the Worshipful Company of Drapers, presented to
Huddersfield Chamber of Commerce.
5. Institute of British Carriage and Automobile Manufacturers Second Prize
Silver Medal, awarded to Rippon Brothers of Huddersfield for "Large
Enclosed Bodywork" in the Private Coachwork Competition, Olympia,
London, 1933.

tokens were purchased in advance by the General Post Office and were marked 'GPO'.[15] Huddersfield Corporation employees used tokens marked 'Departmental'. Prepayment tokens become increasingly popular in the twentieth century, and were used in Huddersfield until the end of 1964.

Shops and Shopping
The earliest unofficial coins from the Huddersfield area are the trade tokens issued in the 1660s during a period of shortage of official small change. Since this scarcity seriously affected everyday transactions by small traders, they issued their own copper or brass coins, in penny, halfpenny or farthing values. This has been suggested as the origin of the phrase 'not worth a brass farthing'. When enough tokens had been collected they could be returned to the issuer who would exchange them for the equivalent in coins of the realm. Issuers in this area were John Dixon (1667), Nicholas Greaves (1668), and Francis Horne (1669) of Almondbury, George Dixon (1666) in Honley and Holmfirth, Edmund Walker (1666) of Huddersfield and John Dyson (1670) in Slaithwaite (Figures 3.4-7). Note that more tokens were issued in Almondbury than in Huddersfield, reflecting the importance of the two villages at this time, before Huddersfield outstripped its rival in the Industrial Revolution of the following century. A halfpenny bearing the name of Richard Kippax of Marsden, formerly attributed to the Colne Valley, is now thought to be from Marsden in Lancashire.[16]

Little research has been done on the issuers of these tokens, although Nicholas Greaves is known to have been a shopkeeper. Sometimes a trade can be guessed from the devices chosen for the token. For example, a pair of scales on John Dixon's token probably denotes a grocer, and Horne's use of the Drapers' Company arms shows his trade. George Dixon's choice of a barrel and Dyson's device of a man with a gun over his shoulder and a dog at his heels both suggest inn signs. Walker's token preserves the old spelling of 'Huthersfield' for Huddersfield, and Dyson's spelling of 'Slaughwhitt' is closer to the local pronunciation still used, of 'Slowitt' than to the official spelling Slaithwaite. These early tokens were being collected as curiosities less than a hundred years after their issue, as is shown by an entry in the diary of Arthur Jessop, an apothecary of New Mill:

> *17th September 1739. I gave Joseph Woodhead a halfpenny for one of Nicholas Greaves of Almondbury's Halfpennys which was coined in 1668 when shopkeepers had liberty to coin halfpennys.* [17]

Although most seventeenth century tokens were round, Greaves

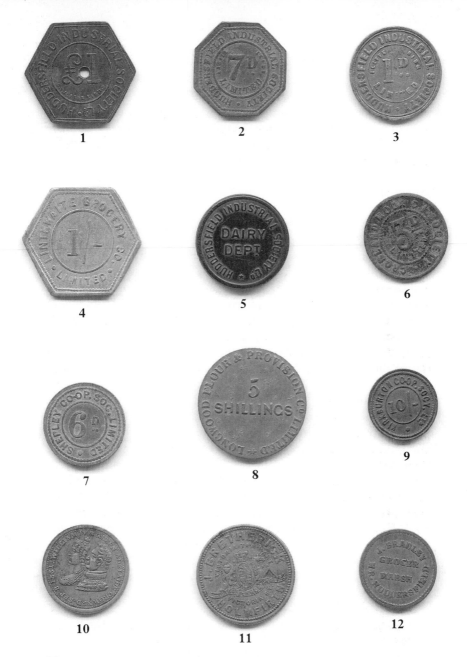

Figure 9:

1. £1 dividend check for Huddersfield Industrial Society.
2. Sevenpence dividend check for Huddersfield Industrial Society.
3. One penny dividend check for Huddersfield Industrial Society.
4. One Shilling (twelve pence) dividend check for Linthwaite Grocery Co Ltd.
5. One pint milk prepayment check for Huddersfield Industrial Society.
6. Threepence dividend check for Crosland Moor Co-operative Industrial Society.
7. Sixpence dividend check for Shepley Co-operative Society.
8. Five shillings dividend check for the Longwood Flour and Provision Company.
9. Ten shillings dividend check for Kirkburton Co-operative Society.
10. Commemorative coronation check issued in 1831 by Labrey and Co., grocers of Market Place, Huddersfield.
11. Advertising check issued by J Bretherick, Victoria Tea Mart, Holmfirth
12. £1 check issued by J Bradley, grocers of Marsh.

chose a heart shape for his, which no doubt added to the attraction for Jessop.

In the 1790s another shortage of official copper coinage prompted a further issue of trade tokens. However, this time only one type was struck for a Huddersfield tradesman, a halfpenny for John Downing, a tea dealer and grocer. Downing issued tokens in 1792 and 1793, (Figure 3.8) with the appropriate designs of the arms of the Grocers' Company and a view of East India House, the London headquarters of the Honorable East India Company, whose ships carried the tea from India and China.

Although trade tokens were again issued in the early nineteenth century, none was produced by Huddersfield companies. However there are many finds reported in the area of tokens issued by Jackson and Lister, linen manufacturers of Barnsley, which bore the design of a weaver working at his loom. Such a design would have been popular amongst Huddersfield's cloth-workers, and it is probable that these tokens were accepted as currency locally.

Although government issues of small change became more regular during the nineteenth century, occasional issues of tokens continued to occur. These probably had a dual use as advertisements, and to give discounts on the next purchase from the shop, rather than as currency, since they rarely include a monetary value in the design. For example, J Bretherick of Victoria Street, Holmfirth distributed a check (Figure 9.11) proclaiming his Victoria Tea Mart as 'Noted for Superior Teas, Coffees and Spices'. (Figure 9.11) R Labrey and Co. of Market Place, Huddersfield, a branch of a Manchester firm, issued a check in 1831 that also commemorated the coronation of King William IV and Queen Adelaide. (Figure 9.10) J Bradley, (Figure 9.12) a grocer of Marsh, Swifts the Huddersfield chemists, and William Sykes, drapers of Taylor Hill, all issued checks with values on them, and these may have been for some kind of 'dividend' system,

Figure 10: *(Opposite)*
1. 1¹/₂ pence check for the *Travellers Inn*, Nieley, Honley.
2. 1¹/₂ pence check issued by W H Levitt at the *Fox and Grapes Inn*, Lockwood.
3. Refreshment ticket issued by Tom Lockwood at the *Three Crowns Inn* ('Molly Pashley's'), Fenay Bridge
4. 1¹/₂ pence check issued at the *Railway Hotel*, Honley.
5. Twopence check issued by Thomas Iredale at the *Bath Hotel*, Lockwood.
6. Admission ticket issued by John Aspinal at the *Belle Vue Gardens,* Sheepridge.
7. Penny gaming check issued at the Berry Brow Liberal Club.
8. Threepence check issued at the King's Arms, Moldgreen.
9. Renter's ticket for the Theatre Royal, Huddersfield.
10. Medal commemorating the opening of Broadbent's Delph Playground, Longwood in 1897.
11. Mrs Sunderland Competition Silver Medal awarded to Miriam Goldthorpe in 1928 for Vocal Music (Soprano).
12. Prize Medal for the Tong Hand Bell Ringing Competition of 1907, awarded to A Townend of the Crosland Moor team.
13. Membership ticket for the Huddersfield Skating Club.
14. Prize Medal for the Challenge Cup of the Huddersfield Gun Club, won by T H Ramsden in 1889.

1

2

3

4

5

6

7

8

9

10

11

12

13

14

similar to that of co-operative societies.

The most common retail 'coin' was however the dividend check issued by co-operative societies (alternatively known as industrial societies or other variations). (Figure 9.1-9) As in most industrial regions, there were large numbers of these societies in the Huddersfield area, ranging from the Huddersfield Industrial Society with its many branches and specialised services, to the Industrial Society in the tiny village of Holme Bridge.[18] Growing from early nineteenth century working class aspirations for advancement through self-help, the aim of these societies was that members (i.e. customers who actually purchased goods) should benefit from the profits, and not remote or passive share-holders.[19] When a profit-share or 'dividend' was announced, members were paid out according to the amount they had spent during the previous period (Figure 9.1-9). Various methods were used for recording this amount.[20] One of the most popular was to hand out metal checks corresponding to the amount spent. These would then be presented as proof of purchase at the 'divi'. These checks were usually round, but could be other shapes, such as the hexagonal penny to sixpence checks used by Linthwaite Grocery Co Ltd. They always carried the name of the society and a value, but rarely any other device. Often they also bear, in small letters, the name of the maker, such as Iliffe of Birmingham (Crosland Moor Co-operative Industrial Society), or Ardill of Leeds (Hillhouse Perseverance Friendly and Industrial Co-operative Society). The metal is usually either a copper alloy, or various silver or grey-coloured alloys known collectively to numismatists as white metal.

Less common but also used by the Huddersfield Industrial Society were pre-payment tokens. These were bought by customers from their local co-op store, and used to pay for goods delivered to the door. This speeded delivery, and meant that the roundsman did not have to handle cash, reducing the risk of theft or fraud. Before the modern use of the car for shopping, it was very useful to have such staples as milk, bread, and coal delivered daily. At the moment, only bread and milk tokens are known for Huddersfield. To avoid having to issue new tokens each time the prices changed, pre-payment tokens were marked with the quantity of goods paid for, for example '1 QT. LOAF, '½ PT', or in more detail 'Tuberculin Tested 1 Pint Jersey milk' or 'Tuberculin Tested 1 Pint Farm Bottled.' Although some pre-payment tokens are in copper alloy, most are made of coloured plastic, which reduced the weight the deliveryman had to carry.

Leisure and Entertainment

One of the most fascinating types of token coinage is the pub or club check. (Figure 10.1-8) These are usually round, carry the name and the address and the landlord's name of a public house, political or working men's club, or even a temperance establishment, and a value, varying usually from a penny to threepence, and corresponding to the price of different drinks. The uses of these checks were various and often obscure.[21] Some were used as prizes in games. For example, one penny checks for the Berry Brow Liberal Club could be bought by members from the bar at a rate of ten for a shilling (twelve pence), thus yielding a profit for the club; the checks could only be redeemed for drinks at the bar, so ensuring a further profit. (Figure 10.7)

Pubs often offered added inducements to customers in the form of entertainment. This could be something simple such as a bowling alley or the occasional concert, but some had more elaborate attractions on offer. The *Belle Vue* hotel at Sheepridge had extensive pleasure gardens laid out by its landlord John Aspinal in about 1850 (Figure 10.6). These grounds enclosed a dance hall, swings, summerhouses and a bowling green. Regular events included fireworks, donkey rides, freak shows and balloon ascents (followed by parachute descents). (Figure 11) Admission was fourpence on Mondays and Saturdays, and sixpence on Wednesdays ('select nights'). Aspinal issued a check or ticket with his own name and the hotel's name on one side, and a griffin (the crest of the Marquis of Rockingham) on the other. Visitors would have paid their fourpence or sixpence, and received the ticket in return, which would be redeemable for part of its purchase price in food or drink. Another check, that of the *Three Crowns*, (Figure 10.3) makes this explicit by stating on the reverse 'Refreshment Ticket'. This check has no address, just the initials 'T. L.', but it is fairly certain that the pub concerned was the one near Woodsome Hall, commonly called *Molly Pashley's* after an early nineteenth century landlady. The last landlord before it closed in 1880 was Tom Lockwood, hence the initials on the check.[22]

Many other Huddersfield pubs issued checks, and the list is growing as more research is done. The *King's Arms*, Mold Green issued an unusual oval check (Figure 10.8). The *Marsh House Inn*, Marsh (still trading) also had a pleasure ground, and issued a twopenny check in its name, the *Cremorne Gardens* (no doubt named after the famous London pleasure gardens). The *Bath Hotel*, Lockwood, whose landlord Thomas Iredale issued a twopenny check in the 1880s, was built as part of a public baths complex in the 1820s, when Lockwood was a 'spa town' on the outskirts of Huddersfield.[23] (Figure 10.5)

As well as Berry Brow Liberal Club, checks were issued by the Huddersfield Liberal Unionist Club, the Kirkheaton Liberal Club and the Moldgreen Working Men's Club. In Victorian Britain, pubs and clubs offered not only drink, but also entertainment, warmth, light and well-cooked food, at a time when many people's houses lacked all these amenities. The temperance movement recognised these needs whilst deploring their association with alcoholic beverages and consequent high levels of drunkenness and domestic violence. Supporters of temperance therefore set up establishments that offered some of the amenities of the public houses but sold only non-alcoholic drinks such as tea, coffee and sarsaparilla. The

Figure 11. Advertisement for an event at the Belle Vue Gardens, Sheepridge in 1890.

Huddersfield Coffee House Company operated three such houses in the 1880s, and issued a check stating that it was 'Good for One Pennyworth of Refreshment'.[24]

Before the advent of the cinema every town had at least one theatre, used for plays, concerts, circuses and other live entertainment.[25] Regular theatre-goers could rent a box for the season, and were issued with a metal ticket of admission. The Tolson Museum collection contains a ticket issued by the Theatre Royal to Mr H C Carr in the period about 1880-1920 (Figure 10.9). Another Theatre Royal ticket, thought also to be for the Huddersfield theatre of that name, admits the bearer to the 'Gal' (gallery).

Many private clubs and societies produced their own prize medals, or preserved prizes won at competitions. Music-making, for which Hudderfield is still famous is represented by a group of medals won by the Crosland Moor Hand-bell Ringers, internationally-renowned champions at the turn of the century.[26] (Figure 10.12) Perhaps more famous is the Mrs Sunderland Competition. Mrs Sunderland of Brighouse (1819-1905) the 'Yorkshire Queen of Song' was a public singer who had performed in front of Queen Victoria. The competition in her honour was first held in 1889, with a silver medal as a prize for vocal music. The number of medals, for various types of musical excellence, quickly expanded. The competition is still held in Huddersfield. The Tolson Museum holds the medal awarded to Miriam Goldthorpe for soprano singing in 1928. (Figure 10.11)

The Museum also contains numismatic evidence for diverse pursuits, such as a prize medal of the Huddersfield Curling Club (1902-3), a metal membership ticket for the Huddersfield Skating Club (Figure 10.13), and the Challenge Cup medal given by the Huddersfield Gun Club to T H Ramsden in 1889 (Figure 10.14). A more recent 'token' is the ticket or souvenir given at the Primrose Hill Free Treat in 1957. The treat started in 1920 and included the crowning of the Rose Queen, a procession around the district with stops for singing songs (especially the Treat anthem *Blossom Bells*), followed by tea, evening games and other entertainments.

Conclusion

It is hoped that this chapter has demonstrated how small and sometimes unimpressive pieces of metal that look like coins can often bear witness to fascinating aspects of past life in Huddersfield. The Kirklees Community History Service continues to collect these tokens, checks and medals for the whole of the Kirklees area, and would like to hear from anyone with actual examples, or information about them or their issuers. The Service's collection is held at the Tolson Museum, Huddersfield, and those parts not on display can be seen by appointment.

Further Reading

Brook, R *The Story of Huddersfield*, 1968.

Edge, B *The First Dictionary of Panumismatica*, 1991.

Haigh, E A H *Huddersfield: a most handsome town*, 1992.

Meldrum, P T *'Co-operative Societies' and Private Traders' Dividend Checks, Prepayment tokens and Club Change' Transactions of Yorkshire Numismatic Society*, 2nd series II (V), 1973 pp.26-35.

Rains, D R *Catalogue of Co-op Checks and Tokens*, 1997.

Rumsby, J H 'Yorkshire Checks and Passes in the Kirklees Museums', *Yorkshire Numismatist* 3, 1997 pp. 211-233.

Teasdill, G *Coin Finds of the Huddersfield district*, 1961.

Whiting, J R S. *Trade Tokens: A Social and Economic History*, 1971.

Notes and References

1. This and other coin finds are listed with references in Teasdill, 1961.

2. For the rise of the Ramsdens, see Whomsley, D and Haigh, E A H, 'The Ramsdens of Longley 1530-1690' in Haigh, 1992 pp. 37-63.

3. Sykes, J *Slawit in the Sixties*, 1926, pp.139-141.

4. The celebrations are described in great detail in the *Huddersfield Examiner*, 26 June 1897 (also reprinted as a pamphlet).

5. The medal is illustrated in Berry, R P *A History of the Formation and Development of the Volunteer Infantry from the earliest times illustrated by the Local Records of Huddersfield and its vicinity, from 1794 to 1874*, 1903, p.364 and pl. opp. p.374.

6. Illustrated in Rumsby, J H 'Attentive Soldiers and Good Citizens': Militia, Volunteers and Military Service in the Huddersfield District 1757-1957' in Haigh, 1992, p.156

7. O'Connell, J 'From Mechanics' Institution to Polytechnic : Further and Higher Education, 1841-1970' in Haigh, 1992, pp. 561-596.

8. Huddersfield Technical School and Mechanics' Institution *Official Catalogue of the Fine Art and Industrial Exhibition*, 1883.

9. Lee P H *The Story of Five Huddersfield College Medals* (1940); Law, E J *Huddersfield College Prize Medals*, (n.d.; typescript in Tolson Museum records).

10. Prospectus of Huddersfield College, 1843 (Tolson Museum Collection).

11. The Dartmouth medal is illustrated, with a list of winners, in Hinchliffe, G *A History of King James's Grammar School in Almondbury*, 1963. Lists of winners of this and other school medals are painted on boards in the classroom known as 'The Big' at the school. I am grateful to Mrs Green, School Secretary, for this information.

12. For details of local pits, see Holmes, D H *The Mining and Quarrying Industries in the Huddersfield District*, 1967.

13. A list of local exhibitors and medal winners at the Great Exhibition of 1851 is printed in Crump, W.B. and Ghorbal, G *History of the Huddersfield Woollen Industry*, (1935; reprinted 1988) pp. 128-132.

14. W C Holmes and Co. Ltd. *Training and Education Offered to Apprentices*, 1917, p.17. The medal is illustrated on p. 19. The Tolson Museum contains a proof striking of the silver medal, hall-marked 1917-1918.

15. Brook , R *The Trolleybuses of Huddersfield*, 1976, p.123.

16. *Yorkshire Numismatist* 3, 1997, pp.105-106.

17. *Three Huddersfield Diaries* (Tollhouse Reprint: l990), p.54.

18. Balmforth, O *The Huddersfield Industrial Society Ltd.: A History of Fifty Years Progress 1860-1910*, 1910

19. Thornes, R 'The Origins of the Co-operative Movement in Huddersfield: the Life and Times of the 1st Huddersfield Co-operative Trading Association', in Haigh, 1992, pp. 171-188.

20. See for example Earnshaw, T *A Short History of South Crosland and Netherton Co-operative Society Limited*, l929, pp. 20, 24.

21. Thompson, R H and Wager, A J 'The purpose and use of public house checks' *British Numismatic Journal* 52, 1982, pp. 215-233.

22. *Huddersfield Examiner*, 18 April 1933.

23. Clarke, B *The History of Lockwood and North Crosland*, 1980 p. 139.

24. Moffat, J P 'Yorkshire Temperance Establishments - Part I' *Yorkshire Numismatist 1*, 1988, pp. 61-70; *Huddersfield Weekly Examiner*, 2 February 1957.

25. For a general account of Huddersfield's theatres, see Chadwick, S *'Theatre Royal' : the Romance of the Huddersfield Stage*, 1941.

26. See the *Huddersfield Examiner* 16 February 1998 for a photograph of Almondbury United Handbell Ringers wearing similar medals whilst on a tour of the United States.

2. THE MANOR OF HONLEY AT WORK 1784-1881

by John Goodchild, M. Univ

THE MANOR OF HONLEY POSSESSES a story which is of perhaps more than local interest, in that working papers as well as formal court records survive in the writer's collection to illustrate its unusually wide range of surviving activities until the court ceased to meet from 1881. Honley Manor's courts supervised a variety of local government functions far beyond the normal period of effective collapse of most manorial administrations.

The purpose of this essay is to study local manorial administration in the period of a century (1780-1881) which the papers happen to cover. The manor covered the area of the township of Honley, of some 2435 acres; by 1781 it was already an area whose inhabitants were primarily concerned in textile manufacture and agriculture, and its population was to grow from 2509 in 1801 (476 families in 446 inhabited houses) to 5584 in 1851, then to decline somewhat and to reach 5070 in 1881. Honley lies on the western side of the river Holme, looking to its market town of Huddersfield some 3½ miles to the north, to which it was connected by a turnpike road (Act 1831) and a railway opened in 1850.

Honley was owned by a number of freeholders but the Earls of Dartmouth owned the manorial rights as well as property in the township. The Dartmouth estates in the West Riding were extensive, extending in 1873 to a total of over 14,723 acres, with a gross estimated rental of a very substantial £26,539.9.0. The earls themselves were non-resident, apart from an occasional temporary residency at Woodsome Hall. Their estates were well – and even benevolently – managed.

The administration of the Dartmouth estates was in the hands of a local agent, William Elmsall, until his dismissal in 1804. He was replaced by London agents who worked through local agents in the West Riding. The holding of manorial courts was a matter for the employment of a lawyer. In 1782 the lawyer Edward Sykes of Dewsbury held the Honley courts (and the Dewsbury Rectory Manor courts); he died in 1804 aged 74. He was followed by his son, also a lawyer, Francis Sykes, who died in 1809 aged 47. The courts then passed into the hands of John Carr, a Wakefield lawyer who also held the Earl of Dartmouth's courts of Slaithwaite cum Lingards and Kirkheaton, and remained in the hands of his successors in his practice at Wakefield. Indeed, it was one of the latter-day partners in that business who gave the surviving records of the manor of Honley, to the present writer, the late S G Beaumont, DL, of Wakefield. John Carr was a nephew of the great Yorkshire architect of that name. He was succeeded in his manorial duties of Honley, following his death in 1824, by his son Robert (who died in 1848 aged 43), by his partner John Nettleton (died 1856 – he was Steward, and then by purchase, Lord of the Rectory Manor of Wakefield). S F Harrison (1805-92) was appointed Steward of the Honley Court and held the last court ever held there in November 1881. The names of these men must be mentioned, as the papers show that not only did they organise and hold the manorial courts, presiding over them, but also they became intimately acquainted with the people of Honley, and with Honley's needs that the court served.

The earliest of the surviving papers are dated 1781 and relate to the decision of a majority of the freeholders of Honley at a public meeting there in 1781 (after considering the matter since 1780) to apply to Parliament for an Act

> *for dividing, inclosing and improving the several Commons and Waste Grounds within the Manor of Honley, in the Parish of Almondbury, in the County of York, and for settling certain Rights or Claims between the Lord of the said Manor and the Freeholders thereof, or some of them.* (Figure 1)

Figure 1. Application to Parliament for the inclosure of land in Honley, 1781

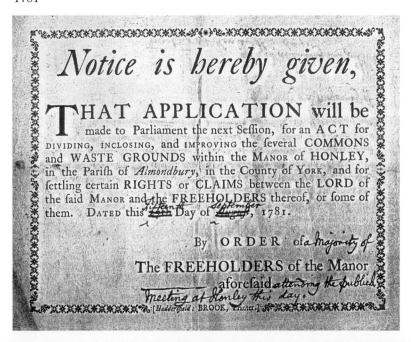

The Act was duly obtained, in 1782, dealing with some 1400 acres, and the necessary legal document, giving title to the newly enclosed plots on the commons, was signed in 1788.

The manorial records as such begin in 1782 and come up to 1881. They cover so wide a field that it is best to discuss the concerns of' the manorial court of Honley under a variety of headings, and subject-wise, rather than purely chronologically.

Administration

The Honley court was a full manorial court, a *court leet* with view of frankpledge,[1] (which was formally the Crown's court) and a *court baron* – the lord of the manor's own court. These were held together as was usual, but in the case of Honley there were, at least by the end of the eighteenth century, no properties whose titles were transferred actually in the manor court – no copyholds.[2] But there were large numbers of those who were obliged legally to attend the Honley court. In 1839, for example, 1100 summonses to attend the court were filled up and signed by the Lawyer–Steward and sent to the manor's bailiff and by him distributed to all residents. In 1841 1200 summonses to the court were filled up and a few days later 200 more, but in 1821 only 800 had been required.

Fines for non-attendance were imposed. Apologies for absence were acceptable; a ten-shilling fine for non-attendance without due cause or apology was made in 1800, in 1806 a fine on three men of 6s 8d apiece was lessened by the affeeror or assessor to the court, to 2s 6d. For refusing to attend, a substantial fine of £5 was imposed (reduced by the affeeror to a still hefty guinea). Two men were fined for insolence in open court, on another occasion a few were 'very saucy'. The whole court worked on the basis of the locals knowing that if they did not attend, or if offences were found to be proven, certain fines would be imposed. The income from these fines was the principal source of court finance, but in fact records show that the cost of holding the courts was always greater than the income.

The courts were held yearly, usually in October (but occasionally slightly earlier or later) until 1863. 1864 was perhaps significantly the year in which the Honley Local Board was established, and thereafter courts were held (of which records survive) in 1865 and 1866, 1874 and finally in 1881. The court was held before the Steward, who swore in a jury, foreman and twelve male jurors. No women were involved although of course there were some women property owners. The court met at 11 am, and a dinner was provided at the cost of the lord of the manor.

In 1798 the refreshments cost

19 dinners	*£ 0. 19. 0*
(presumably for jurors and court officials)	
punch	*£ 1. 11. 0*
ale and tobacco	*£ 0. 7. 0*
horse hay and corn (for those who used horses)	*£ 0. 2. 0*
servants	*£ 0. 2. 0*

In 1814-18 the courts and the dinners were held at the *Wheatsheaf Inn* (Figure 2) and printed billheads survive. In 1814 a typical public house bill from William Theaker showed

eating	*£1. 15. 0*
punch	*£0. 15. 0*
ale and porter	*£0. 5. 0*
servants eating & ale	*£0. 5. 0*
horses' hay and corn	*£0. 2. 10*

In 1859 Timothy Bamforth provided the accommodation and dinners, and in 1874 the *Coach and Horses* provided the hospitality.

The manorial income included small sums of between 3d and 28 shillings, which were payable yearly as free, quit, or chief rents by (in 1830 for example) 24 freeholdings. These were often more than a couple of decades in arrears, although supposed to be paid at each

Figure 2. *Wheatsheaf Inn*, Southgate Honley. *Kirklees Cultural Services*

court meeting. As properties were divided (and amalgamated) these sums remained the same. They could be bought out, and in 1789 two Honley merchants bought out a total of five such rents at thirty years' purchase.

It was the Steward of the manor who had the most responsible duties. Early in the nineteenth century he charged two guineas for attendance, plus his travelling, his administrative expenses (printing, postage, letters and so forth). The Steward normally stayed at the *George* in Huddersfield, holding his courts at Honley, Slaithwaite cum Lingards and Kirkheaton on successive days. A deputy steward and a seal is mentioned in 1800, and deputy stewards were also appointed in 1874 and 1881, being then partners in the steward's law business in Wakefield.

There was a written ritual for the Steward in holding the annual court itself, and copies of this survive. It included a fairly detailed address to the jurymen detailing their duties and it is in fact one that was commonly in use in manorial courts. The Steward was assisted by a paid bailiff in the court, who also collected the fines imposed, circulated the notices of the court's meeting, served warrants to levy fines on debtors' goods if fines were unpaid and assisted generally. The other court officials, all of course part time, were the township's constable (chosen by the inhabitants but sworn in at the Court), his deputy, two byelawmen (who saw to the implementation of decisions and to the manorial weights and measure jurisdiction), the affeeror, a pinder who saw to straying livestock, and the manorial gamekeeper (this last was an appointment for years rather than an annual one). Sometimes the officials annoyed the court, as when in 1802 the constable and his deputy and the byelawmen were all fined a substantial £5 apiece for neglecting their duty, although the affeeror reduced these hefty sums to 2s 6d (5 shillings for the constable). Breach of the pinfold was a major offence: in 1798 three men were fined for a 'rescue' from the pound. In 1860 Frederick France of Honley was appointed by the court both pinder and public bellman.

Public Health

The court was much concerned with the maintenance of a sanitary state within the township by the prevention of 'nuisances' which threatened the status quo. It had no right (or finance) to improve matters other than by removing threats to public health. In 1782 wool, yarn, skins etc., any containers or barrels, were not to be washed in Honley Town Wells so preventing the cattle drinking there (Figure 3). In 1802 dyewater threatened the public drinking supply, and in 1808

Figure 3. Towngate, Honley. *Kirklees Cultural Services*

dyewater was allowed onto the public highway and the threat of a 40 shilling fine imposed (Figure 4).

In 1854 the town's sewage was fouling the public watering place at Great Spout and a fine of £5 was threatened unless all was cleared away in fourteen days. As with other courts, the lord of the manor himself was dealt with if necessary, and in 1830 Lord Dartmouth had been found to be not restraining a watercourse in Honley, and it was found at the court that the necessary work had not yet been done. The offence of obstructing a watercourse was common, and could bring a substantial £2 fine.

In 1829 it is recorded that one man's manure was draining into another's cowhouse and in 1830 the sewers in two yards required repair and a potential fine of £5 on each threatened. Dirt, blood and filth from a dunghill opposite the *George and Dragon* were dealt with

Figure 4. Bottom of the Gate, Honley. *Kirklees Cultural Services*

in 1836. It was not solely a matter of reporting troubles: sometimes the jury would go out to see for themselves. In 1853 the jury went to view the way to the spring in Hawk Royd Bank Wood, where working the stone had made it almost impossible to get to and use the spring; 53 persons had raised the issue. In 1850 there were two privy nuisances and the drainage of water from two properties was unsatisfactory. A manure heap needed to be removed from the roadside and the walls round Scotgate Head Quarry to be repaired. Wells in Moll in the Wood required repair as did railings in front of Stockwell Row. In 1851 the postmaster of Honley reported to the court the 'filthy and impassable State of Cow Lane' leading to Honley Station which he had to travel, with danger, four times a day.

Any inhabitant of the township could raise a matter with the court by letter or verbally. The good and great did not escape notice as we have seen with Dartmouth himself. When Brook & Sons were raising their dam by some two feet and were leading stones for the purpose, putting Steps Mill into backwater, the jury again had to see for themselves. Many such matters occur – some as simple as when in 1834 one man laid manure against another's door. Others as serious as six butchers who in 1881 were providing a weekly nuisance.

Highways

Roads of all sorts – except apparently turnpike roads – were the concern of the court. Obstruction of footpaths and highways, not keeping the gates, roadside trees and hedges, ditches, and fences in repair; the court was even willing to take the case to the Quarter Sessions if necessary. In 1836 New Street in Honley required its roadway repaired, the responsibility of the township Surveyors of Highways; a fine of £20 was laid if the work was not done and the Petty Sessions magistrates at Huddersfield would also be asked to intervene. The Honley court was certainly a robust one.

In 1806 a new building being erected at Mag Bridge caused a public nuisance, and was in any case an encroachment according to the old men who gave evidence before the court. Mag Bridge was a ruin in 1824. In 1808 there is recorded a trespass where the court decided that there is no public footpath. A property owner complained of the condition of Neeley Road and Cow Lane in 1828. The court ordered that two men should examine the footpath for about a mile between Factory Gate and the east end of Magwater Bridge and report its state in 1828, while in 1839 the footpath up the side of Cliff Wood was 'almost past Getting up or down'. 'A very serious nuisance' to those using the footpath to Steps Mill appears in 1839. A footpath was stopped because the new railway had not built a bridge. In 1852 a bridge was destroyed by 'a late flood' – the Holmfirth Flood. (Figure 5)

Quarries

As well as the fencing of quarries where public danger was concerned, the court held a protective brief against outsider users. In 1808 stone obtained from Slate Pit Quarry had been sold to a Meltham man and a fine of £2 was imposed; another man 'got' two cartloads of stone in Scott Gate Quarry. Presumably these were township quarries; Scott Gate Quarry certainly was one, as it is set out at the inclosure. In 1815 a warrant to raise £10 by the sale of a man's goods was issued by the court in regard to stone illegally got from there. In 1847 there is a note in regard to 1889 loads of stone sold from Dartmouth's Hagg Wood Quarry to the road surveyors of Honley and Netherthong, for which one penny a load was due. In Little Hagg Wood, the court found in 1848 that three men had each illegally grazed five cows, and fined them.

In 1854 the court decided that two men form a committee to see to the carrying out of the findings of court and assist the byelawmen in their duties – which were effectively to carry out the court's decisions. But the court had its own occasional troubles as when in 1848 one man refused to pay his fine as (it was claimed) 'Thomas Bradley of Huddersfield puts those persons up to it to refuse to pay or do any thing therefore we must do something'.

Weights and Measures

One of the most unusual survivals in the Manor of Honley was the jurisdiction, actively exercised, over the sale of foods and consumable liquids. It was not unique, as a similar authority was exercised in the neighbouring and far larger Manor of Wakefield. The collapse of manorial jurisdiction at Honley may have been due to the national legislation leading to the removal of such concerns to a county level.

In 1802 reference occurs to the Honley jurisdiction over weights, measures, a balance and packs of meal. In 1803 two women and three men were fined between ten and forty shillings (affeerored to 2s 6d to 30s) for their possession of weights which were not accurate, and four men were fined for using half peck and half quartern measures which provided insufficient measure. The numbers who offended in such ways were considerable: in 1806 ten men were found to use short weights and two short measures.

In 1839 – and these are but some from among continuing references – a manorial court warrant was issued to summon two men, 'to hear a charge to be made against them' for short weights and unfair scales. A customary tenant of the manor, a Honley shopkeeper, refused to show his weights to be checked by the byelawmen of the manor in 1843. In 1845 a Honley innkeeper refused to produce his spirit measure to the byelawmen and in 1846 a butcher there refused to give up what had been found to be a short weight contrary to the custom of the manor.

The account for inspecting the weights and measures was as usual sent to the Steward in 1840 and the manorial measures included a strike, peck and quartern measures made of wood, with copper

Figure 4. Magdale, Honley, 1952. *Huddersfield Examiner*

fittings. When the standard set of the weights of the manor were stamped as accurate they consisted of weights from one quarter of an ounce to four pounds, with a set of scales, beam and box, and a box for the whole.

In 1843 a legal Case for the Opinion of Counsel was prepared as to the powers of the West Riding's own inspectors to survey those of the manor of Honley. In 1856 the Honley measures (all made of wood) ranged from quart, to half gill, half bushel, peck, half peck, quarter and eighth peck. They were no longer regarded as sufficient standard measures and, for Government verification, must be cleared of all earlier stampings and have the names of the manor, Riding and county engraved upon them. The steward was informed that a set of

replacement gunmetal measures would cost £21, plus a bushel measure at some £16, and an imperial standard yard measure made of brass and in a mahogany case, three guineas. Only a couple of months later, in November 1856, de Grave & Co of London supplied Honley with three boxes containing all the new equipment needed. The wooden measures had been checked and all found incorrect, with uneven top edges; these were ground down and stamped at the London Guildhall as being correct in capacity. Interestingly, weights in Honley were assessed as ounces, sixpences and pins – a quarter ounce weighed two sixpences and thirteen pins, and a sixpence weighed 25 pins, so there were 252 pins to the ounce.

The weights and measures legislation of 1859 and 1878 reserved rights in such matters already exercised by manorial courts leet and other individuals, or bodies, but the Honley jurisdiction slipped away.

The Honley Court probably also concerned itself with licensing. The court papers contain a certificate of the township constable and householders from 1827 that states that J P Osborn of Honley, 'hitherto an Excise Officer there', was a fit person to be landlord of the *Coach and Horses* 'at the bottom of the Gate in Honley'. Also included is the associated licence of the magistrates.

Generally

The draft of the Honley court record of the annual court, held in October 1782 in the presence of the Steward, bailiff, thirteen jurymen, constable and his deputy, two byelawmen and pinder, had illustrated the concern of the court with the continuing provision of pure water, the prevention of getting stone in the commons and the preservation of the boundary walls of the commons, the prevention of woodcutting from the commons and the maintenance of public ways. These and the range of matters mentioned already in this essay continued to be the court's active concern until its last meeting in November 1881. The Honley manor court had done an important and a useful job; now the job became that of a more modern type of local government, but one which was no more representative, and perhaps little more efficient, than the ancient one.

Glossary

1. Frankpledge : The corperate responsibility for the good behaviour of others.
2. Copyhold : Tenure of land – less than freehold – evidenced by a copy of the Court Roll.

3. THE WHOLE HOG - HUDDERSFIELD CHARTISM 1838-1855

by Alan J Brooke

ON 26 SEPTEMBER 1838, in the Social Institute, Manchester Street (the Socialists' meeting room), a committee convened to establish the Huddersfield Northern Union (NU), modelled on the Great Northern Union founded in Leeds by Feargus O'Connor, to promote the People's Charter. Its members were veterans of a decade of struggle for parliamentary reform, the free press, the ten hour day, and trade unionism. Their most recent and bitter campaign, until only a month before led by Richard Oastler, was against the implementation of the New Poor Law with its 'bastille' workhouses.[1]

Among them were Joseph Thornton, a Paddock cloth dresser, chair of the Oastler Testimonial Fund; the Scot, Lawrence Pitkethly of Buxton Road, a shawl draper active in every field of Huddersfield working class politics since the late 1820s; Chris Tinker, Republican, beerseller and newsagent of Market Walk, imprisoned two years before for selling unstamped (i.e. untaxed) newspapers; John Hanson, leading Owenite Socialist and factory reformer; Samuel Binns, wool sorter and Stephen Dickinson, cloth dealer of King Street, all leading anti-Poor Law campaigners.

They called a public meeting the following week at Kay's Room, Bull and Mouth Street, which was crowded 'to suffocation' while hundreds more clamoured to get in. Aready the NU had enrolled 256 members. The National Petition and the People's Charter were formally adopted and organization begun for the Great West Riding demonstration to be held on the common at Peep Green (Hartshead Moor) on 15 October. Proudly the local correspondent reported to O'Connor's *Northern Star*,

> *In a few days we shall stand first in the list - the place where Huddersfield has always stood in the principles now advocated.*[2]

Those principles were emblazoned on a large green silk banner displayed by the Huddersfield contingent on the march to Peep Green,

> *Universal Suffrage is a Birthright and We Will Have It - Taxation without Representation is Tyranny and Shall Be Resisted.*

The villages of Honley, Linthwaite, Yew Green, Lepton, Newsome and Almondbury were also represented among the crowd which was conservatively estimated at 50,000. It was from the impoverished handloom weavers of such villages and hamlets, who for more than twenty years had waged a struggle against industrial capitalism and undemocratic government, that Huddersfield Chartism drew its radicalism and vitality. Pitkethly announced that some Huddersfield workers had been threatened with dismissal if they came to Peep Green. Already nationally renowned, he was elected as a West Riding delegate to the National Convention, planned to oversee the presentation of the Petition and Charter to parliament (Figure 1).[3]

Pitkethly also chaired a meeting held after the large torchlight procession on 3 November that escorted O'Connor from Honley Bridge to Holmfirth in torrential rain. Over the following months, according to the *Star*, 'long slumbering, Whig ridden Holmfirth', was added to the areas where the collection of signatures for the Petition and funds for the 'National Rent' to maintain the Convention was proceeding apace. At the West Riding delegate meeting at the *Black Bull*, Liversedge, on 28 January, £26.11s was paid in from the Huddersfield area out of a total of just over £200.[4]

Alarmed by the growing support for the Charter, the Whigs attempted to tap discontent for their own class interests. A meeting to establish a local Anti-Corn Law Association (ACLA) was called by 151 merchants and manufacturers for 29 January 1839. The chairman William Brook, millowner and magistrate, overruled a motion by Sam Binns linking the abolition of the Corn Laws to universal suffrage. By pasting 'Poor' over 'Corn' on the advertisements for the next meeting, the Chartists helped ensure it was packed with sympathizers and one, William Stocks a former Constable, was in the chair. John Hanson accused the Whigs of raising the repeal of the Corn Laws as a diversion from the Charter, while Tom Vevers condemned those now seeking workers' support as the very men responsible for the, 'manufacturing hells where your wives and children are ground down'. Sixty-three years old Vevers, an active radical for over forty years, had been implicated in an attempted uprising in 1817. He remained one of the most popular local Chartists up to his death in 1843.[5]

While the Convention deliberated, it became evident that the government would ignore the Petition. Repression of the Chartist movement seemed imminent. In May some pistols were defiantly discharged as an angry crown gathered in Northgate around a newly posted proclamation prohibiting arming and drilling. Despite the town being placarded with magistrates' warnings against unlawful

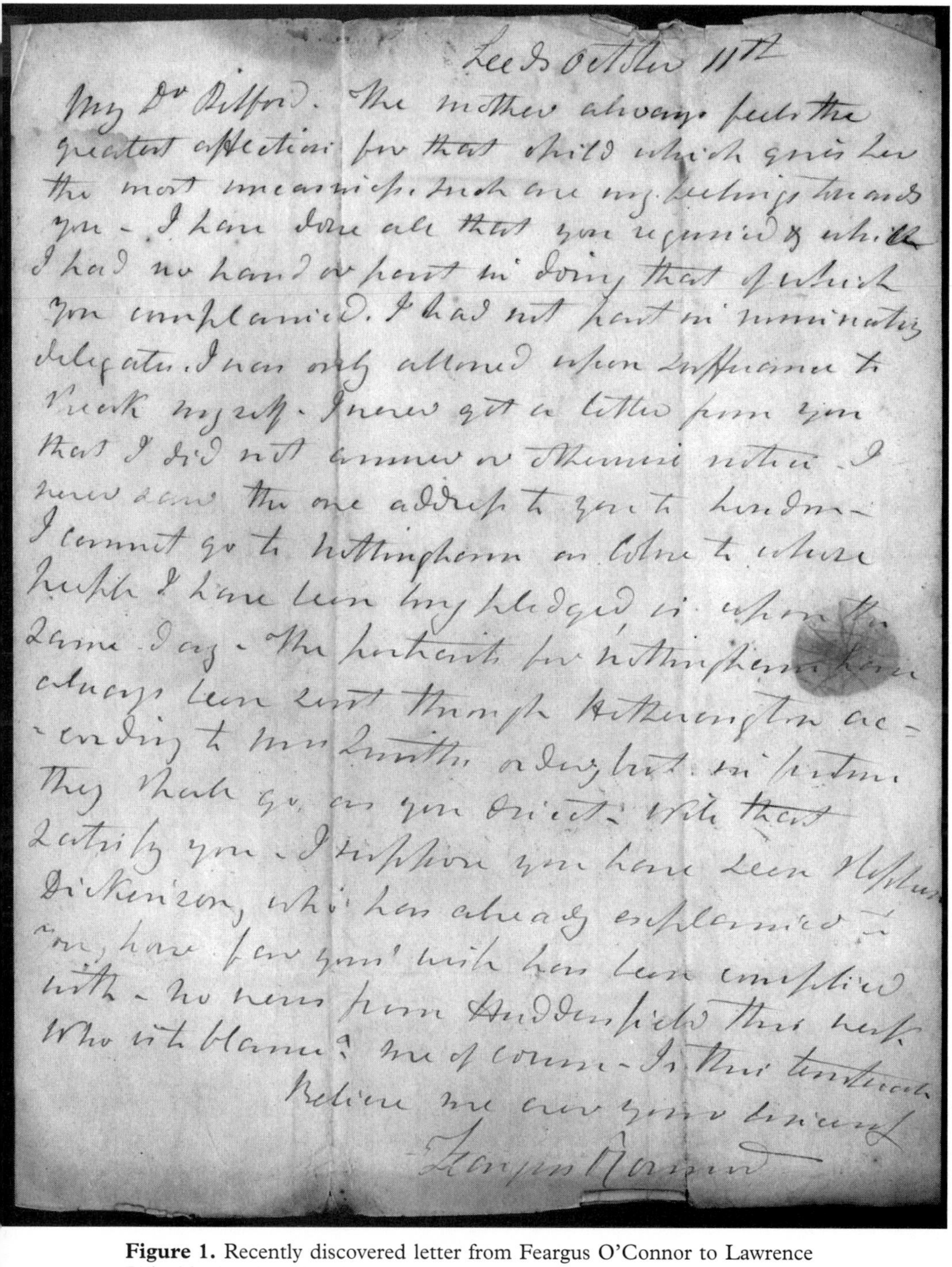

Figure 1. Recently discovered letter from Feargus O'Connor to Lawrence Pitkethly dated 11 October 1838, denying he had interfered with Pitkethly's nomination as delegate. *Kirklees Cultural Services*

meetings, George Barker, a co-operative society enthusiast, chaired a protest against O'Connor's prosecution for libel (regarded as an attempt to silence the *Star*), and the 'tyrannical' measures directed against the Chartists.[6]

In this tense atmosphere, despite more magisterial threats, one of a number of simultaneous nation-wide Whit-Tuesday demonstrations was held at Peep Green. Vevers stated defiantly, 'they would defend their liberties to the death, always taking care to stand by the laws', a sentiment echoed by O'Connor who affirmed, 'should they employ force against us, I am for repelling attack by attack.' Anxiety about a clash with the authorities may have reduced attendance – an informer claimed that the Huddersfield area's turnout was 'the poorest thing there ever has been'. Although they were employing at least two informers, John Brown, a Huddersfield fancy weaver, and John Clough, a labourer from Taylor Hill, the magistrates were unable to report any evidence of planned insurrection more sinister than daggers displayed in Tinker's shop window.[7]

Huddersfield NU eagerly adopted the Manifesto of the Convention, in a declaration which revealed that enthusiasm had indeed been flagging,

> *Huddersfield is again beginning to bestir itself and show to the oppressors of the poor that where necessity requires the spirit of freedom is deeply engrafted in the bosom of the industrious labourer...hoist the cap of liberty.*

A few weeks later, after an 'animated discussion', 40 cordwainers joined. Yew Green Working Men's Association also announced that membership was increasing, even from the 'valley of poor Whig-ridden Lockwood.' Collections for National Rent and the Defence Fund for prosecuted Chartists were pursued with renewed energy.[8]

The Manifesto proposed the adoption of a series of 'ulterior measures' should the petition for the Charter be rejected, including a run on the banks, abstention from taxed goods and, most revolutionary, a 'Sacred Month', or general strike, set for 12 August. Vevers was elected as a reserve delegate to the Convention, in case of the arrest of the sitting ones. Pitkethly, meanwhile, was one Member of the Convention beginning to have doubts about the feasibility of the strike, warning, 'if the people made a struggle when they were unprepared to sustain it they would only rivet their chains faster as the French did...' On 5 August, in Dickinson's room King Street, Huddersfield NU discussed the issue at length and adopted a resolution by Barker, *that until the ulterior measures recommended by the Convention as set forth in the manifesto have had a fair trial and the productive classes are better organized and united and Ireland aroused from its slumbers, it would be unwise to commence the Sacred Month, seeing the improbability of getting the factory hands in this district to make a general stand.*[9]

On 10 August a meeting was held on Back Green to protest at a police attack on Chartists at Birmingham Bull Ring. Attendance was poor, perhaps as low as 300, partly due to lashing rain but also in response to an intimidating proclamation from the magistrates. Barker called for support for the ulterior measures and William Martin a Bradford Irishman, warned against secret conspiracies that would provide the excuse the government wanted to arrest Chartist leaders. Dickinson closed the meeting on a slightly ominous note, announcing to cheers, 'Those that stood in the rain will be able to stand something else if necessary'. Locally, only Almondbury observed the Sacred Month, now modified to a three day holiday, which left only one in ten looms in the village working.[10]

The failure of the ulterior measures produced a sense of anti-climax and despondency. The *Mercury* revelled in the Chartists' supposed disappointment '...that Huddersfield from being a seat of turbulence should have become a sample of peace and good citizenship.' Organization appears to have deteriorated to such a degree in Huddersfield that in one week in September no order was received for the *Star* and the following month Honley was warned that without cash in advance their papers would not be delivered. It was becoming increasingly difficult to find meeting rooms. Huddersfield Chartists were barred from using the Philosophical Hall (Figure 2).[11]

Moral persuasion had proved ineffective, many Chartists were in gaol and the trade depression had deepened. It is not surprising that some considered turning belligerent words into action. But there is no evidence that Huddersfield Chartists were involved in the insurrectionary movement. Pitkethly was in contact with the south Wales leader, John Frost, as early as July and may have known of the armed preparations to free Henry Vincent in Newport. An informer also implicated him in the aborted January rising when Chartists in Bradford, Dewsbury and Sheffield gathered under arms. While he was at the Heckmondwike meeting on 4 October, where the plot was supposed to have been hatched, there is no evidence that this was other than a routine West Riding delegate meeting.[12]

The Huddersfield Chartists expressed sympathy with the insurgents

Figure 2. The Philosophical Hall, Ramsden Street, scene of anti-poor Law 'riot' in 1838, was the venue for many Chartist political and social events. The building was converted to a theatre in 1864 and destroyed by fire on 16 February 1880. *Kirklees Cultural Services*

but at least in public statements, did not condone their methods. Protesting in January 1840 at the conviction of the Welsh rebels, William Cunningham of Holmfirth, an Irish weaver, told the meeting that Frost's, 'only object was to make a moral force demonstration in favour of Vincent'. While Barker warned that the rising in Sheffield was more likely to get the prisoners hanged than released. Nevertheless, local Chartists also supported the Sheffield prisoners. Pitkethly wrote to John Duffy in Northallerton gaol and funds were raised for the family of John Clayton who died there.[13]

In May, news of O'Connor's imprisonment in York Castle ran through the district like an 'electric shock'. In one protest, twenty-eight block printers at Dewhirst's, Aspley, collectively signed a pledge of abstinence until his release. They had already sent a collection to the Defence Fund for prisoners.[14]

By early April the district showed signs of revitalization and, in June, it was agreed to send a delegate to Manchester to discuss national reorganization. There was still a strong sense of frustration with the methods being employed, expressed by Honley NU in an open letter to O'Connor, signed by the secretary Chris Wood.

We had a petition got up to sign and can assure you that the people here are completely tired of signing petitions and say they will sign no more nor ask a favour for anything at our legislators' disposal, but are determined to have their rights conceded to them if possible at all hazards...our blood boils in our veins with revenge... [15]

The Manchester meeting on 20 July founded the National Charter Association (NCA), intended to give more cohesion and central direction to the movement. A committee was soon formed in Huddersfield with a twenty two-year-old tailor, Edward Clayton, as chairman, and an appeal issued, 'To the Working Men of Huddersfield and the surrounding Neighbourhood'

Awake! Awake! Arouse ye from this apathy! Cast off this slumbering delusion and come forward in the glorious cause of freedom...ye that were wont to be foremost in the fight...

concluding with the slogan: 'Universal Suffrage and No Surrender.'

Huddersfield was divided into 'classes' and a 'large number' of new members enrolled, while an out-township delegate meeting was held to form committees, sign-up members and appoint missionaries to the villages. The revival was boosted by the visit of the recently released Peter McDouall and John Collins, who were escorted into town on 5 September by a massive crowd with bands and banners. Even the *Leeds Times* reporter concluded, 'We never saw a more animating or successful demonstration of public feeling.' Applause rolled from street to street and around 1200 crowded into a meeting in the Socialists' Hall of Science on Bath Street (Figure 3).[16]

By October Huddersfield NCA had around 200 members and lectures were planned at Almondbury, Kirkheaton, Honley and Slaithwaite, 'Thus the progress of the Charter will be demonstrated throughout the whole district.' Activity was soon progressing 'at almost railway speed', with the forming of classes in the out-townships. The former radical strongholds and predominantly fancy weaving areas, were again the most prominent.[17]

Figure 3. The Hall of Science, Bath Street, built by the Socialists in 1839. The scene of meetings addressed by national Chartist leaders including O'Connor, O'Brien and Vincent. Rooms were regularly let to the Chartists in 1844. *Kirklees Cultural Services*

But there were signs that the unanimity behind the O'Connorite strategy was cracking. In November Almondbury NCA discussed the necessity of the union of the middle and working classes to obtain universal suffrage. On Christmas Eve veteran Almondbury radicals, John Buckley, Sam Dickinson and George Beaumont debated the issue with Huddersfield NCA members, including the clothdresser James Shaw of Marsh and Clayton, who argued that 'the labouring classes of themselves are quite competent to work out their political regeneration.' Although the discussion was conducted 'in good humour' there was a 'little party feeling' evident.[18]

External opposition also increased in late 1840 with the founding of an ACLA for 'operatives'. Huddersfield NCA responded with a meeting to counterpose the merits of the Charter to Corn Law repeal. In January 1841 the president of the NCA Executive, James Leach of Manchester, condemned the divisiveness of 'the cry of cheap bread' in a debate with the ACLA lecturer J Finnegan. ACLA manufacturers retaliated by denying Chartists meeting rooms, William Brooke, preventing a lecture in the Guild Hall.[19]

At least in Huddersfield that summer the rivalry was not as bitter as Manchester, where ACLA manufacturers used Irish supporters of Daniel O'Connell to break up Chartist meetings. A NCA outdoor meeting in a yard at Upperhead Row to protest against the Manchester 'bloodies' was attended by local O'Connellites, led by 'Red Tempest' and 'Skilly Broadley', but they did not intervene as speakers condemned events in Manchester and ended with three cheers for O'Connor and the Welsh patriots.[20]

Pitkethly was put forward as Chartist candidate in the West Riding elections alongside George Julian Harney. The famous 'Paddock Bastille Flag' which had seen action in the 1837 election in support of Oastler, was brought out for the hustings in Huddersfield. Some stone throwing occurred when Whig horsemen rode into the Chartists. The Chartists marched to the nomination meeting at Wakefield where Wood of Honley proposed Pitkethly. His support in the show of hands equalled the Whig candidates' but the poll was not contested. Compared to 1837, when two people were killed in Wakefield, it was a peaceful campaign, although the Whig column suffered some stoning on the return to Huddersfield.[21]

After the election Harney toured the Huddersfield area warning that the Chartists could expect nothing better from the new government, reminding them of the 'dark, despotic and bloody deeds of the Tories'. Other speakers of national renown who visited Huddersfield later that year were Henry Vincent and Bronterre O'Brien, who spoke at the

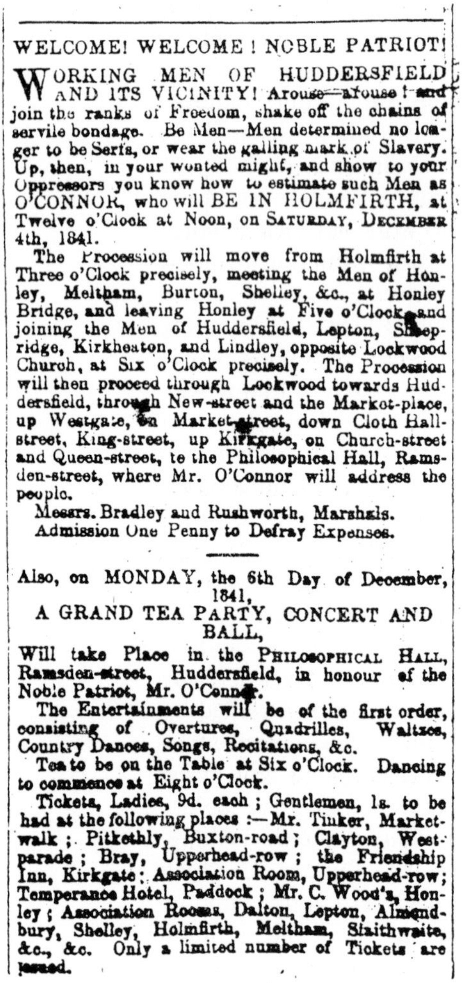

WELCOME! WELCOME ! NOBLE PATRIOT!

WORKING MEN OF HUDDERSFIELD AND ITS VICINITY! Arouse—arouse ! and join the ranks of Freedom, shake off the chains of servile bondage. Be Men—Men determined no longer to be Serfs, or wear the galling mark of Slavery. Up, then, in your wonted might, and show to your Oppressors you know how to estimate such Men as O'CONNOR, who will BE IN HOLMFIRTH, at Twelve o'Clock at Noon, on SATURDAY, DECEMBER 4th, 1841.

The Procession will move from Holmfirth at Three o'Clock precisely, meeting the Men of Honley, Meltham, Burton, Shelley, &c., at Honley Bridge, and leaving Honley at Five o'Clock, and joining the Men of Huddersfield, Lepton, Sheepridge, Kirkheaton, and Lindley, opposite Lockwood Church, at Six o'Clock precisely. The Procession will then proceed through Lockwood towards Huddersfield, through New-street and the Market-place, up Westgate, on Market-street, down Cloth Hall-street, King-street, up Kirkgate, on Church-street and Queen-street, to the Philosophical Hall, Ramsden-street, where Mr. O'Connor will address the people.

Messrs. Bradley and Rushworth, Marshals.

Admission One Penny to Defray Expenses.

Also, on MONDAY, the 6th Day of December, 1841,
A GRAND TEA PARTY, CONCERT AND BALL,

Will take Place in the PHILOSOPHICAL HALL, Ramsden-street, Huddersfield, in honour of the Noble Patriot, Mr. O'Connor.

The Entertainments will be of the first order, consisting of Overtures, Quadrilles, Waltzes, Country Dances, Songs, Recitations, &c.

Tea to be on the Table at Six o'Clock. Dancing to commence at Eight o'Clock.

Tickets, Ladies, 9d. each ; Gentlemen, 1s. to be had at the following places :—Mr. Tinker, Market-walk ; Pitkethly, Buxton-road ; Clayton, West-parade ; Bray, Upperhead-row ; the Friendship Inn, Kirkgate ; Association Room, Upperhead-row; Temperance Hotel, Paddock ; Mr. C. Wood's, Honley ; Association Rooms, Dalton, Lepton, Almondbury, Shelley, Holmfirth, Meltham, Slaithwaite, &c., &c. Only a limited number of Tickets are issued.

Figure 4. *Northern Star* 27 November 1841 advert for events starring Feargus O'Connor.

Hall of Science, and James Duffy who recounted his experiences in 'the hell hole' of Northallerton gaol.[22]

The year culminated in a visit from O'Connor who was honoured with a procession down the valley from Holmfirth to a rally in the Philosophical Hall on Saturday 4 December and a 'Grand Tea Party, Concert and Ball' on the following Monday. The popularity of O'Connor is evident from the number of local children named after him. John Dyson, fancy weaver, of North Green, Almondbury; Duke Hinchliffe, labourer, Paddock; John Milnes, fancy weaver, Lascelles Hall and James Thornton, cloth dresser, Lords Mill, are just some of those who have infants called Feargus, or even Feargus O'Connor, in the 1841 census (Figure 4).[23]

A township delegate meeting on 26 December decided to employ a full time lecturer and an Irishman, George Condy, was soon appointed. His efforts in early 1842 proved satisfactory as the movement was 'progressing' in areas like Holmfirth. Huddersfield reported to the January West Riding delegate meeting that all its debts were clear. As well as the 4d per member levy to maintain the lecturer, money was being raised for another Convention on which Pitkethly again sat, although it was a much smaller, low-key affair than 1839.[24]

Chris Wood, facing debtors' gaol after being sacked for nominating Pitkethly at Wakefield, resigned as district secretary on 27 March, and was replaced by Edward Clayton. Among the towns and villages now represented at delegate meetings were Huddersfield, Almondbury, Kirkheaton, Lepton, Paddock, Dalton, Shelley, Skelmanthorpe, Stocksmoor, Thurstonland, Holmfirth, Honley, Meltham, Berry

Brow, Yew Green, Slaithwaite and (Upper or/and Nether) Thong. There was also a NCA at Newsome. The number of members is impossible to ascertain. Between March 1841 and October 1842 Huddersfield took out 630 membership cards, although all may not have been issued.[25]

The *Star's* publication of 'Nominations to the General Council' provides 74 names of local NCA council members. As would be expected, all but one, (an engineer), in Lepton, Almondbury and Kirkheaton are weavers; in Holmfirth nine out of ten are clothiers while in Lockwood/Yew Green there are two cloth dressers, a clogger, a cotton spinner and two smiths, including David Gledhill. Huddersfield is the most diverse, with two packers, two tailors a shopkeeper, a newsagent (Joshua Hobson) and Tom Vevers as 'gentleman'.[26]

Although it is known that women were involved in collecting signatures and funds, attending meetings and demonstrations and that Kirkheaton NCA even had female members, the name of no local female Chartist seems to be recorded. There is one misogynistic description from the Whig *Leeds Mercury*, of a Holmfirth Chartist, likening her to an 'Amazon' or character from *Macbeth*, allegedly living on Jamaica rum and brown stout, earned by her 'shoeless, stockingless, shirtless factory children.'[27]

Discontent at Parliament's rejection of the second Petition was fuelled by increasing unemployment and wage cuts. Sunday 'Camp Meetings', modelled on those of the Methodists, began on Castle Hill. On 13 July an estimated 15,000 converged on the hill to hear David Ross. Two weeks later Dickinson was speaking on 'unequal distribution and class legislation'. While these meetings showed the Chartists could mobilise 'swarms of people', a spontaneous popular movement outside of their control suddenly dwarfed their efforts (Figure 5). [28]

Beginning on Friday 12 August strikers – men, women and children – poured over the Pennines, down the Holme and Colne Valleys into Huddersfield, gathering local support en route. Almost every workplace in the area was stopped and on Sunday many were injured when Lancers charged the crowd in the Market Place. Numerous rank and file Chartists joined the strike, but the response of Huddersfield NCA Council, like the national leadership, was confused and vacillating. Although at a mass meeting on Back Green local strikers proposed to cheers, 'We'll join you for the Charter', Huddersfield NCA published a statement disassociating itself from the movement,

> *The riots neither originated with, nor have they been participated in, by the associated body of Chartists, whatever may have been the*

conduct of a few individuals bearing the name.

The role of some of these individuals was dredged up later. Edward Clayton was charged in 1844 by the *Star* (which condemned the strike as Anti-Corn Law League plot) with,

> *horrible conduct during the "Plug Plot" riots of 1842, by which you sought to produce CONFUSION in your native town (against the repeatedly expressed will and wishes of the Chartists of the District) and through which you nearly betrayed innocent but confiding men...*

This may be related to an incident where a bill sticker was arrested for posting a militant placard, (possibly the Declaration of the National Executive, which belatedly backed the strike), leading to raids on two Chartist newsagents. As late as 1858 David Gledhill was accused of having, '...made an oration to the 'Plugites' in 1842 and then hid himself – determined not to die a martyr'.

The failure of the NCA to give leadership in the strike, and the ensuing repression and demoralisation, proved a turning point for Chartism.[29]

One immediate threat was successfully countered. The Complete Suffrage Union (CSU), a creation of the Anti Corn Law League, which aimed at creating a diluted Chartism more acceptable to the middle classes, had tried to establish a Huddersfield branch in March. Clayton and Shaw persuasively swung that meeting behind 'nothing short of the whole Charter'. In October the founder of the CSU, Joseph Sturge, spoke at the Guildhall, inspiring the *Leeds Times* to

Figure 5. Castle Hill, Almondbury, before the tower was built, much as it would have appeared to the thousands of Chartists who gathered for meetings in the 1840s. *Alan Brooke*

claim the CSU was 'making rapid progress among the electoral classes of Huddersfield'. Suggestions that Huddersfield NCA was about to compromise with the CSU over choosing delegates to the December Conference in Birmingham alarmed the editor of the *Star*, who lamented that Huddersfield Chartists, 'have hitherto always been considered up to the mark'. At the selection meeting the Chartists demanded three of the four places for Shaw, Cunningham and Clayton. The CSU delegate refused to attend on these terms and his place was taken by Vevers.[30]

Attempts were made at reorganisation in early 1843 but continued stagnation was still evident at the Honley delegate meeting in July which cheerily reported 'brightening prospects' and expectations that,

> *The lull caused by the strike-plot will soon again be succeeded by the healthy breeze of Legal Agitation – in the worst of times there are a gallant little few who cannot be forced to abandon the cause...*

Camp Meetings were resumed on 13 August, firstly on Castle Hill, despite some interference by the authorities, who ordered the closure of all the beerhouses for miles around, and, on the following Sunday, near Holmfirth. The *Mercury* dismissed the attendance at Castle Hill as only 'a little remnant of this once popular faction'. At the end of the month the NCA issued a reminder that it still met every Tuesday evening in the Chartist Rooms, Upperhead Row, but reported optimistically that several new members had been recruited,

> *...it is hoped the slumbering energies of Chartism in this neighbourhood will once more be roused. Time was when this locality was considered one of the strongholds of Chartism...*

The Socialists, who were in even deeper political and financial crisis, agreed in January 1844 that the Chartists could use the Hall of Science on alternate Sundays and two nights a week.[31]

The economic depression of the 1840s spurred some workers to look for a more immediate solution to poverty and insecurity, rather than awaiting political reform based on the Charter. This mood influenced even the 'whole hog' O'Connorites. Some, like John Chapman, an ironmoulder, involved themselves in trade unionism, while the *Star* itself actively promoted support for striking miners. Other panaceas were more individualistic – even escapist.[32]

In the summer of 1842 Pitkethly visited America where he met a number of former radicals from the Huddersfield area. The following year the *Star* serialized his account of conditions in the States, intended to assist emigration. Pitkethly, (who appears to have played little part in local Chartism after his return), ran a branch of the British Emigrant's Mutual Aid Society from his shop, as did a Huddersfield grocer, Jabez Todd. Another prominent local activist to set sail in 1842 was Chris Tinker, on a mission to reconnoitre the site for a Socialist community. He died two years later in Milwaukee.[33]

In February 1843 a public meeting on economic distress attended by Vevers, Pitkethly and Robert Owen called for a scheme 'to establish the unemployed upon the land'. This was a plan also being promoted by O'Connor in a pamphlet, *The Management of Small Farms*, which called, not for Socialist communities, but for estates of independent smallholdings. Readings from this were held in December at Almondbury NCA meetings. Honley NCA called for halfpenny a week levy to buy land and tools, 'as an asylum' for those who lost their living advocating the cause, and the July district delegate meeting also called for 'a practical experiment upon the land'.[34]

O'Connor's Chartist Co-operative Land Society was launched at a Convention in April 1845. In June, at Turner's Temperance Hall, Chapel Hill, the Huddersfield District Committee of the society was formed and twenty-six shares subscribed for. Huddersfield initiated a meeting of Yorkshire societies at Dewsbury on 26 October that advised registration under the Benefit & Building Societies Act. Within weeks, however, Huddersfield Co-operative Land Society was at loggerheads with O'Connor. The omission of a resolution from the *Star's* report of a further Dewsbury meeting and O'Connor's failure to acknowledge money which had been paid in, caused umbrage. The *Star's* claim that Huddersfield members feared a Socialist take over of the land movement may be an allusion to Joshua Hobson, who was still involved with the Owenites. Hobson had rowed with O'Connor and resigned as publisher of the *Star* after its removal from Leeds to London. Having taken over Tinker's newsagents and library, he returned to his native town. He was elected Huddersfield delegate to a Manchester Land Conference in December, although members must have been aware of the friction with O'Connor.[35]

Hobson had his own model farm at Birkby, where his achievements included raising a thirty-eight stone pig. Chartists also visited another experimental farm at Paddock, run by the cloth dresser Joseph Thornton, an acknowledged authority on the use of sewage fertilizer and the effects of industrial pollution on plants.[36]

There were over 264 shareholders of the Land Company (as it was now called), in Huddersfield, Holmfirth, Clayton West, Almondbury and Lepton, most of them weavers/clothiers. At least three of these were settled on the land by 1848. Eli Sikes was allotted four and Duke

Denton two acres on the Charterville estate at Minster Lovell. John Bradshaw of Almondbury left a thirty shilling a week job to buy his plot but soon fell into debt. Huddersfield also sent a delegate, John Gledhill, to the Conference at the Lowbands estate in 1847.[37]

Hobson was also at the centre of controversy in the NCA. In April 1844 a row between the supporters of Hobson and of Clayton over the election of conference delegates, led to their ejection from the room at Upperhead Row. A meeting was convened at the Hall of Science, 'to consider the treacherous conduct pursued towards the district by some of the members', and Chartists at Lockwood called for an investigation into charges against Clayton levelled by O'Connor. He was accused not only of misdemeanours during the 1842 strike, but also of financial irregularities. The splits were eagerly seized on by the CSU that claimed to be making 'decided progress' in Huddersfield.[38]

In 1846 the *Star* described the town as the 'headquarters' of anti-O'Connor forces, condemning recent intrigue as the worse 'of all the low, of all the mean, of all the rascally attempts at mischief recently made at Huddersfield.' But, by now, there was only 'A little remnant of Chartists that still survive in Huddersfield...' according to the *Mercury.*[39]

The French revolution of 1848, unrest in Ireland and trade depression stimulated a brief resurgence. William Murphy, chair of a Chartist meeting on repression in Ireland in late 1847, was elected delegate to the Chartist convention in April where he enthusiastically claimed that his constituents, 'were resolved to have the Charter, morally if possible, but to have it any road...'. Joseph Barker, a former Methodist, was elected as reserve delegate at a meeting chaired by Clayton, apparently back in the saddle.[40]

A Huddersfield Reform Association meeting on 5 June passed 'by an overwhelming majority' the proposal of Murphy and others for 'whole hog' reform based on the Charter, followed by three cheers for O'Connor and the Irish felon John Mitchell. On 25 June a Castle Hill demonstration was held, but the *Mercury,* estimating the crowd at 5000, commented, 'it was creditable to the working men of Huddersfield that but few of their numbers attended.' The following month, after police prevented another assembly on Castle Hill, people gathered at Armitage Bridge to hear David Lightowler, a Bradford Chartist later convicted of drilling men on Tong Moor.[41]

Huddersfield remained untouched by the disturbances in places like Bradford, Bingley and Ashton. 'The Chartists at Bradford', gloated the Tory *Leeds Intelligencer*, 'appear quite indignant at the peaceful behaviour of their Huddersfield brethren and accuse them of cowardice...' By September the *Mercury* pronounced Chartist agitation in Huddersfield, 'entirely defunct', and although their were rumours of secret arming and drilling, police raids only recovered a few old guns in two Chartist homes at Almondbury Bank and Longley Hill.[42]

The Chartists fielded a candidate in the December West Riding elections when Richard Brook, a bookseller of Buxton Road, moved the nomination of Samuel Kydd at Wakefield, but the campaign had none of the vitality of 1841.[43]

The following year little activity was reported other than the 'limited attendance' at a camp meeting on Joseph Barker's farm at Crosland Moor. Apart from visits by Ernest Jones, the Chartist candidate for Halifax, and the sending of delegate Tom Hirst to the 1851 Convention there was little effort to reorganise Chartism until 1855. That July a meeting on the fairground at the back of Buxton Road chapel condemned Palmerston and the war in the Crimea and called for reform based on the Charter. The posters advertised the event as, 'The Dead Alive Again', prompting the *Huddersfield Examiner* to remark, '...if Chartism be alive again it is very weak and feeble...'. The resurrection was so weak in fact that Chartism, as a movement, did not outlast the year.[44]

Stalwarts kept the banner flying. David Gledhill, at a parliamentary reform meeting in 1858, proposed universal suffrage, asserting, 'the labouring classes have been forty years in advance of the middle classes in political knowledge'. Although only twenty hands were raised for his resolution - and two years later he was shouted down altogether – he and other veterans continued to demand votes for workingmen through the reform campaigns of the 1860s and 1880s. Their ideas lived on into the twentieth century, in the struggle to extend those rights to working class women.[45]

Notes and References

1. This chapter is adapted from Brooke, A J *The Social and Political Response to Industrialisation in the Huddersfield Area c.1790-1850* unpublished PhD thesis (1988), Chapters VI-VIII, particularly pp 359-457, (available in Huddersfield Local History Library). I would like to thank the staff of Huddersfield Local History Library (HLHL) and West Yorkshire Archive Service (Kirklees), in particular, Lesley Kipling, for assistance during this research. One of the most recent, and best, works on the background of Chartism is Thompson, Dorothy *The Chartists* (New York 1984).
2. *Northern Star* (NS) 29 Sept; NS 6 Oct 1838.
3. *NS* Extra Supplement 16 Oct 1838.
4. *NS* 10 Nov 1838, *NS* 2 Feb 1839.
5. *Leeds Mercury (LM)* 2 Feb 1839, 9 Feb 1839; *NS* 9 Feb 1839; *Leeds Times (LT)* 9 Feb 1839; *NS* 27 May 1843.
6. *LT* 11 May 1839; *NS* 25 May 1839.

7. *NS* 25 May 1839; Home Office. (HO).40/51, Laycock (clerk to the Huddersfield magistrates) to Home Office 22 May 1839; ibid: Joseph Armitage to HO. 14 Feb 1839.

8. *NS* 6 Jul, 20 Jul, 27 Jul, 3 Aug 1839.

9. *NS* 17Aug 1839

10. *NS* 17 Aug 1839: *LM* 17 Aug 1839; HO.40/51(375) Brook, Starkey and Sutcliffe, magistrates, to Home Office 10 Aug 1839; HO.40/51 (453) Transcript of meeting sent by Harewood. Back Green was at the end of Queen Street, where the ring-road now is.

11. *LM* 24 Aug; *NS* 21 Sep; *NS* 9 Nov; NS 16 Nov 1839.

12. Frost to Pitkethly 12 Jul 1839 (Pitkethly collection, HLHL). For the 'conspiracy' see Hovell, Mark *The Chartist Movement*, MUP 1966, p183; Peacock, A J. *Bradford Chartism 1838-1840* (York 1969).

13. *NS* 21 Dec 1839, NS 1 Feb 1840. Pitkethly's letter is quoted in Ward, J T *Chartism* (London 1973) p247.

14. *NS* 30 May, 13 Jun, 27 Jun, 4 Jul, 1 Aug 1840.

15. *NS* 20 Jun 1840.

16. *NS* 15 Aug, 12 Sep 1840; LT 12 Sep 1840.

17. *NS* 3 Oct 1840.

18. *LT* 2 Jan 1841.

19. *NS* 5 Dec; 12 Dec; 24 Dec 1840; 2 Jan; 16 Jan; 1841.

20. *NS* 19 Jun 1841; LT 19 Jun 1841.

21. *NS* 10 Jul 1841; LT 26 Jun; *Halifax Guardian* (HG) 3 Jul 1841.

22. *NS* 7 Aug; 16 Oct 1841; 6 Nov 1841; LT 30 Oct 1841.

23. *NS* 11 Dec 1841. Other names include John Feargus Fielding (Huddersfield Chronicle 5 Jan 1867); Feargus Firth *(Huddersfield Weekly Examiner (HEW)* 20 Jun 1874); Feargus O'Connor Kitson, *Huddersfield Directory* 1900, Ash St, Halifax Old Rd, who is probably the Feargus Kitson, nightsoil man in HEW 12 Oct 1878). Feargus, the son of John Milnes, appears in the 1871 Census aged 32, coalminer.

24. *NS* 1 Jan; 8 Jan; 22 Jan - 26 Feb 1842. Pitkethly appears to have had little support from Huddersfield, having only 37 votes to Binns 115 and Clayton's 121, NS 5 Mar 1842.

25. *NS* 14 May 1842; Epstein, J. *The Lion of Freedom* (1982) p231-232 for note on estimating membership from cards issued.

26. *NS* 12 Feb, 26 Aug 1842, Yew Green, 10 Dec 1842, Yew Green and Lockwood; 19 Feb 1842, Newsome; 26 Feb 1842, 7 Jan 1843, Honley; 5 Mar 1842, Lepton; 22 Oct 1842, Almondbury; 26 Nov 1842, Holmfirth; 17 Dec 1842, Huddersfield; 31 Dec 1842, Kirkheaton.

27. *NS* 12 Nov 1842; LM 23 Feb 1839

28. *NS* 9 Jul, 6 Aug 1842.

29. *NS* 20 Aug 1842; LM 20 Aug 1842; NS 4 May 1844; *Huddersfield Examiner* (HE) 18 Dec 1858.

30. HG 5 Mar 1842; *LM* 5 Mar 1842; LT 24 Oct 1842; *NS* 10 Dec 1842; *LT* 24 Dec 1842.

31. *NS* 29 Jul 1842; NS 19 Aug 1842; LM 19 Aug 1842; *NS* 2 Sep 1842; *NS* 24 Jan 1842.

32. *NS.*27 Apr 1844; NS 6 Jan 1844 et.seq.

33. *NS* 8 Apr 1843 et seq; Brook, Michael. 'Canadian Revolutionaries in the United States' in *Ontario Historical Society* Vol. LVII No.2 June 1965. I am indebted to Michael Brook for a copy of Chris Tinker's son's account of emigration to America.

34. *NS* 25 Feb 1843; NS 2 Dec 1843; *NS* 15 Jul 1843.

35. *NS* 21 Jun 1845; NS 18 Oct, 15 Nov ; 22 Nov 1845.

36. *LM* 21 Nov 1846; NS 18 Oct 1845, Thornton was also proposed for the Board of Directors of the CCLS, NS 15 Nov 1845.

37. Thompson, D, *op.cit.* p217; *NS* 13 Mar 1847; *LM* 21 Oct 1848, Hadfield, Alice M. *The Chartist Land Company* (Newton Abbot 1970) pp 160-161. Nearly thirty years later, John Arlom of Lepton recollected visiting Minster Lovell with his father, but they apparently did not take a plot, *HEW* 10 Aug 1872; *NS* 21 Jul 1847.

38. *LT* 13 Apr 1844, *NS* 13 Apr, 20 Apr 1844; NS 4 May 1844, Hobson backed O'Connor's accusations. LT 1 Feb 1845.

39. *NS* 8 Aug 1846; *LM* 7 Feb 1846.

40. Gammage. *History of the Chartism Movement 1837-1854* (Merlin Reprint 1876); *NS* 18 Dec 1847; *NS* 15 Apr 1848; *LI* 15 Apr 1848

41. *LM* 10 Jun 1848; *LM* 1 Jul 1848; *NS* 19 Aug, *LM* 12 Aug 1848; *LI* 20 Dec 1848.

42. *LI.*3 Jun 1848; *LM* 9 Sep 1848; *LM* 16 Sep, *NS* 23 Sep 1848.

43. *LI* 11 Dec 1848.

44. *LM* 16 Jun 1848; Gammage *op.cit.* p307 HC 3 Jul 1852; *HE* 31 Jul 1855.

45. *HE* 24 Dec 1858; *HC* 30 Mar 1861.

4. Susan Sunderland: 'The Yorkshire Queen of Song'

by John A Hargreaves

DURING HER PROFESSIONAL CAREER, which commenced at Deighton an industrial hamlet near Huddersfield, in 1833 and concluded at an emotional farewell concert at the Philosophical Hall in Huddersfield in 1864, Susan Sunderland, a former textile worker, earned the soubriquet, 'the Yorkshire Queen of Song'(Figure 1).[1] She became the toast of Victorian England for her powerful soprano solos from Handel's oratorios such as 'I know that my redeemer liveth' and her repertoire of popular vocal melodies such as Sir Henry Bishop's 'Home sweet home'. Although she was born and bred in neighbouring Brighouse, where she married a local butcher, made her home,

brought up her family and died within a stone's throw of where she had been born, she developed a strong association with Huddersfield. Indeed she disclosed, in an interview with John G Schofield for the Huddersfield Choral Society's *Magazine of Music* in June 1889, that she had nowhere met with 'more cordial appreciation than at the Huddersfield Choral Society's concerts' at which she so frequently sang and recalled that throughout her long career 'with but a slight interruption'. She had maintained 'a very intimate connection with the society' of which she had been a founder member, singing principal soprano in the society's first public performance of the *Messiah*. Moreover, her name today is commemorated in the annual Mrs Sunderland Musical Festival held at Huddersfield Town Hall, which commenced in April 1889 at the Huddersfield Technical School.[2]

Figure 1. Portrait of Mrs Susan Sunderland in pastels by Samuel Howell, 1856. *Huddersfield Choral Society*

Susan Sunderland was born on 30 April 1819 at Spring Gardens, Slead Syke, Brighouse, Yorkshire, the daughter of James Sykes (1782-l846), a gardener, and his wife, Hannah (1785-1855), 'humble and respectable' parents, both of whom were 'decidedly musical'. After her marriage to Henry Sunderland (1817-93), a Brighouse butcher and farmer, on 7 June 1838, she moved to the nearby Spring Terrace, Waring Green, Brighouse, which remained her home for the rest of her life. Whilst her husband, Henry Sunderland, was a well-known figure in Brighouse, he never took a prominent part in public life. When he died, aged seventy-seven in 1893 the *Brighouse Echo* reported that he had retired from the butchery trade 'about forty years ago', which would have been around 1853, over a decade before his wife's retirement from her career as a professional singer.[3]

In 1819, Brighouse formed part of the township of Hipperholme-cum-Brighouse, covering an area of 2,550 acres within the ancient parish of Halifax and by 1834 was described in a contemporary directory as 'a populous and rapidly increasing village'. The population of the expanding industrial village doubled from approximately 2,500 inhabitants in 1841 to 5,000 in 1851. Brighouse, with access to convenient turnpike, waterway and rail communications, was considered sufficiently important to have a new parish church erected with assistance from the parliamentary commissioners in 1830-31 at a cost of £3,514 and also had a strong Nonconformist presence, with a well-established Quaker meeting house and new Wesleyan and Methodist New Connexion chapels. In 1846 an act of Parliament was obtained for lighting Brighouse with gas under a body of improvement commissioners. But the emerging urban centre, holding its annual pig fair on 12 October, retained a distinct rural character beyond mid-century and was still designated a 'large and well-built village' in a later directory in 1853.[4]

Susan Sunderland received her earliest musical training from a local blacksmith, Luke Settle, an accomplished flautist, who later became choirmaster of Brighouse Parish Church. He discovered her musical talents by accident around 1831, hearing her singing as he passed by the garden wall of her home at Slead Syke, Brighouse. He reputedly said to the singing girl: 'Tha's gotten a rare voice. If tha'll come down to my place I'll teach thee how to use it'. Her earliest vocal training therefore was received at a blacksmith's forge at Slead Syke, Brighouse, while Luke Settle kept time with his hammer on the anvil. He trained her to breathe deeply, project her voice and enunciate her words clearly. She then realised an early ambition by joining the choir of Bridge End Independent Chapel, Rastrick, where John Denham, the cellist and singer, was choirmaster. She later acknowledged, however, that she owed her greatest indebtedness for musical tuition and success in her profession to Daniel Sugden, a double bass player, who was associated with both the Halifax Choral Society and the Halifax Sunday School Jubilee Sings. The Bradford antiquary, William Cudworth, records that Sugden was 'one of the ablest musicians in

Figure 2. Woodhouse Hill looking towards Christ Church c.1910.
Kirklees Cultural Services

the West Riding', who 'could play every instrument in the orchestra' and was generous in providing tuition for others. He later introduced her to the Halifax Choral Society and obtained engagements for her with the Sacred Harmonic Society.[5]

Miss Susan Sykes, as she was then styled, made her début at the age of fourteen, on Friday 1 February 1833 at the benefit concert of the musical society in the local school room at Deighton, a 'populous' hamlet between Huddersfield and Brighouse, specialising in the

manufacture of velveteen and woollen cords. With its 'beautiful and chaste' new gothic church at Woodhouse, erected ten years earlier by John Whitacre, a local woollen manufacturer, and its thriving Methodist chapel, the hamlet had long been 'identified with choral music' and provided an appreciative audience for the young soprano's rendition of 'Wise men flattering' from Handel's 'Judas Maccabaeus' (Figure 2). Reminiscing in an interview with the *Yorkshire Evening Post* on the eve of her eightieth birthday, she recalled how she had been accompanied by a band from Leeds, conducted by Mr Bywater, who 'had no baton', but 'used to stamp with his feet' to keep time and revealed that she had retained the programme from her first public performance at Deighton as one of her 'most cherished possessions'. The expanding local economy, the increasing propensity for sacred music by church and chapel congregations and the growing popularity of songs and glees provided the context for the launch of her remarkable career. However, she soon developed a marked preference for Handel's oratorios, and 'as these compositions formed the staple of the various choral societies' concert programmes of that day', she devoted herself 'closely to their study', thereby acquiring 'an intense love for the magnificent solos which the great composer wrote for the soprano voice'.[6]

At the opening of the organ at St Paul's Church, Huddersfield in December 1835, she sang 'Rejoice, greatly' from Handel's *Messiah,* accompanied on the organ by Henry Horn, and was subsequently appointed principal treble at St Paul's from 1 April 1836, an appointment which she held for eight years. She also sang on Sunday evenings at Huddersfield Parish Church, whose first organist was the celebrated Thomas Parratt, and with church choirs in Brighouse, and Southowram. The opportunities provided by the liturgical calendar and special events such as the inauguration of a new organ, together with the regular training that she received through her membership of local church and chapel choirs helped to develop her confidence as a public performer.[7]

The lack of educational provision for the children of the poor in the early nineteenth century had meant that her general education, however, had been 'only that of a meagre character' and at the age of sixteen 'her pronunciation and delivery' were considered to be 'of a rude and uncultivated character'. After she had been engaged to sing on the periodical meeting nights of the Ramsden Arms Glee Club, one of the earliest musical societies in Huddersfield meeting in Cross Church Street, she was 'placed under the tuition' of a Huddersfield schoolmaster, Mr Kaye, 'to improve her elocutionary powers' following which 'her style wonderfully improved'. This was reflected in the remuneration that she received for her singing. She received five shillings per night in her first season with the club, ten shillings per night in the second season and subsequently five pounds per engagement (Figure 3).[8]

She became a founder member of the Huddersfield Choral Society in 1836 and was principal soprano, at the age of seventeen in the society's first performance of music from the *Messiah* before a 'numerous and respectable audience' in the infant school room, Spring Street, Huddersfield on 30 December 1836. As a female artiste in the male dominated choral society, only eight of whose fifty-four members in 1837 were women, she was enormously fêted and became the society's 'favourite soloist for many years'. She sometimes received less than flattering reviews, as on one occasion in the 1839-40 season, when her singing was criticised as 'rather sharp' and on 2 April 1852, when she was reported not to have been in such good voice as usual, but was nonetheless loudly applauded. By 1845, she was in such popular demand that the dates of the Huddersfield Choral Society concerts were determined by her availability, but by October 1845, she had left the ranks of the society. Moreover, a letter written to her by John Crosland, secretary of the society, on 26 June 1846 requesting

Figure 3. The first Huddersfield Concert Party: Miss Crosland, Mrs Sunderland, Mr Joe Lister, Mr Ingersoll and Mr Joe Wood. *Mr R Wood*

Figure 4. Mrs Sunderland with Huddersfield Choral Society artistes. Probably at the memorial concert Mr Henry Horn, 20 May 1852. Mrs Sunderland is seated on the left and Miss Crosland on the right. *Huddersfield Choral Society*

the return of music books belonging to the society reveals a degree of friction between the committee of the society and its former principal soloist. A reconciliation appears to have been effected during the following year, when she was again being professionally engaged by the society and her name appears as soloist at its concerts until 1863. Following the death of Henry Horn at the age of fifty-one, she sang at a packed memorial concert to the society's first conductor on 20 May 1852 at the Philosophical Hall in Huddersfield (Figures 4 and 5).[9]

Daniel Sugden reputedly paid her five shillings, early in her career, for singing 'Ye men of Gaza' from *Samson* at a Halifax Choral Society concert, but the archives of the society reveal that her name first appeared on a programme of the Halifax Choral Society in 1839 as a soloist in Handel's *Alexander's Feast*, and she subsequently sang in almost every concert until her final appearance as one of the soloists in *Elijah* in 1863, shortly before her retirement from the professional stage. She occasionally sang with other Halifax musical societies. When the Halifax Philharmonic Society was reconstituted in May 1860, she was invited to sing at its first concert at the Mechanics Institute and appears also to have sung with the Halifax Glee and Madrigal Society in a concert at Belle Vue, Manchester during the same year. She also sang on other special occasions in Halifax, such as the opening of the People's Park on 14 August 1857, when she sang the national anthem as a solo 'before a great multitude'; at a memorial service for James Uriah Walker, the former proprietor of the *Halifax Guardian* at the South Parade Wesleyan Chapel and at the mayor's banquet to celebrate the opening of Halifax Town Hall in 1863, when she sang 'The Captive Greek Girl' by Hobbs.[10]

Her first public appearance in Bradford was at a concert on 19 February 1838 in the Exchange Buildings, Piccadilly and her last official engagement in the town on 11 April 1864 at St George's Hall with the Bradford Festival Choral Society. However, her relationship with the Bradford musical festival proved controversial in the 1850s. She was engaged as a soloist in the inaugural festival which followed the opening of St George's Hall in 1853, but her contribution was limited to the singing of 'If God be with us' from Handel's *Messiah* and a solitary 'air', 'I'm alone', sung at a Miscellaneous Concert on the Wednesday evening. G F Sewell, in his *History of the Bradford Festival Choral* Society states that Mrs Sunderland's scanty recognition at the 1853 festival disappointed her many admirers and she was loudly cheered until she gave an encore of her song at the Wednesday evening performance. At the next triennial festival in 1856, she became the centre of a major row. She had been billed to sing 'If God be with us' from the *Messiah* and was affronted when the

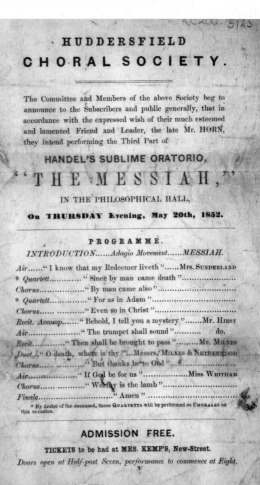

Figure 5. Concert programme for the memorial concert for Mr Henry Horn, 20 May 1852. *Huddersfield Choral Society*

Chairman of the Bradford Festival Committee, Alderman Samuel Smith (1804-73), Mayor of Bradford from 1851 to 1854, requested that the performance of the *Messiah* be shortened and the solo deleted from the programme in order to accommodate other guest performers. An acrimonious correspondence between the alderman and the soprano followed, which Mrs Sunderland published in the press, winning much public sympathy for her treatment. Amends were only made when at a later concert in the newly refurbished Philosophical Hall in Huddersfield on 9 October 1856 a chastened Samuel Smith publicly apologized. Kneeling before her, he begged her forgiveness for

> *a penitent offender who, under the delusions and fascinations of foreign prima donnas, did so cruel a wrong to your talents and your rights.*

Extending her hand towards him, she replied:

> *Rise, Mr Smith. Rise, and be sure that my forgiveness is as frank and as full as your own confession. I declare you again worthy to sit in the chair of vocal and instrumental patronage at St George's Hall*

The extraordinary episode concluded with the reconciled duo singing together the appropriate air 'Auld Lang Syne', in which Mr Smith's deep bass notes gave admirable relief to the fine soprano of Mrs Sunderland.[11]

She sang before Queen Victoria at the opening of Leeds Town Hall on 7 September 1858 and was one of the principal artistes at the first Leeds Musical Festival in 1858 that followed the opening ceremonies, substituting for Madame Weiss. Her appearance was greeted with 'hearty applause' and the 'full volume' of her voice 'as well as mastery in oratorio singing' was shown in the recitative 'Lo, now a slant' and in the following trio.

Following the Leeds Musical Festival, the Yorkshire Choral Union was founded by Mr R S Burton, the talented organist of Leeds Parish Church, who became conductor of the combined choirs. On 26 May 1860 the Yorkshire Choral Union, under the presidency of Sir Peter Fairburn, the Mayor of Leeds, was commanded to sing before Queen Victoria, Prince Albert and King Leopold of the Belgians at Buckingham Palace. Two hundred vocalists from the Leeds Festival Choral Society, the Huddersfield Choral Society and including sixty members of the Halifax Choral Society and the Halifax Glee and Madrigal Society, travelled to London for the command performance in the new ballroom at Buckingham Palace. The Bradford Festival Choral Society had sung at Buckingham Palace in 1858 and the

Halifax Guardian, revealing the intense rivalry which existed between the musical societies in the towns of the West Riding during this period, observed:

> *A year or two ago, Her Majesty honoured the Bradford singers with a command to sing before her, and it was but natural that that section of the Riding should arrogate to itself exclusive glory at this special preference, and should ostentatiously throw off the whole of the musicians of the rest of the Riding.*[12]

Following the performance on the evening of 1 June, 1860, Queen Victoria recorded in her Journal that she:

> *went into the Ball Room, where the Company was assembled. The Yorkshire Choral Symphony sang, and extremely well. It consists of the Leeds, Halifax and Huddersfield Choral Societies.*[13]

Although the surviving transcription of Queen Victoria's journal does not refer to Mrs Sunderland by name, the *Halifax Guardian* reported that:

> *Mrs Sunderland was in splendid voice and the accompaniments to her song were most tastefully played by Mr Burton. One verse of the national anthem, given as a solo by Mrs Sunderland and repeated in full chorus terminated the concert. Her Majesty expressed to Mr Burton the high gratification she had in listening to the splendid and well-trained voices of her Yorkshire subjects.*

The programme, devised by Prince Albert, and preserved in the Royal Archives at Windsor Castle, reveals that Mrs Sunderland's solo, earlier in the evening was 'Oh, bid your faithful Ariel fly', by Thomas Arne (1710-1778), the leading British composer of incidental music for the theatre in his day, including the intensely patriotic 'Rule, Britannia'. The Queen apparently 'bowed her thanks' to the 'famed Yorkshire Queen of Song' after the performance, when 'the chorus enjoyed the hospitality of Her Majesty in one of the adjoining rooms'. The following day the choir presented an entirely different programme at a public performance at the Crystal Palace, when the rain came down in torrents. Mrs Sunderland sang 'The Captive Girl' by Hobbs 'with thrilling effect', a song which she had sung for the Queen 'when she was first honoured with a command to sing in Buckingham Palace', following her moving rendition of the national anthem at the opening of Leeds Town Hall.[14]

She had earned the compliments of the Prince Consort and the Duke of Cambridge eighteen years earlier at her London début at the

Ancient Concerts at the Hanover Square Rooms in 1842 and subsequently sang on a number of occasions in the metropolis with the
Sacred Harmonic Society at concerts in the Exeter Hall. She sang in
the *Messiah* on 2 November 1849 and 22 December 1851 and on New
Year's Eve 1855 sang in the *Creation*. A month later, on 31 January
1856, 'she sang the whole of the soprano solos in *Elijah* with most
distinguished success' and 'the highest critics ransacked their vocabularies
for expressive superlative adjectives'. Following a performance of the
Messiah with the Sacred Harmonic Society at the Exeter Hall on 10
December 1858, her final public appearance in the capital, *The Times*
critic maintained that, with the exception of Clara Novello, there was
no contemporary English singer able to render the soprano music of
the *Messiah* 'so impressively' and commented that 'had she made
London her residence instead of Yorkshire, she would probably long
before this have earned abundant fame in the metropolis'. Another
eminent music critic, George Hogarth, father-in-law of the novelist
Charles Dickens and a former editor of the *Halifax Guardian*,
described her in the *Daily News* as a:

> singer of high attainments, worthy to hold a principal place on any
> metropolitan orchestra. Her voice is a real soprano, at once clear,
> mellow, flexible and delicately in tune ... her performance could scarcely
> have been surpassed by any of our English sopranos, especially her
> rendering of 'Rejoice, greatly'. For a quarter of a century she has been
> a leading attraction in the British Isles and her concerts and concert
> tours in the principal towns have been wonderfully successful. [15]

She sang in Glasgow, Edinburgh, Belfast, Dublin and Aberdeen,
where she was presented by her admirers with 'a very handsome
brooch' before an audience of 3,000 to 4,000, which she wore when
Samuel Howell, the cellist and artist, painted a full-length portrait of
her in pastels in 1856. The painting which shows the singer in middle
age was praised for its 'true to life' portrait with 'the expression of
feature being admirably caught and rendered'. Invariably simply
attired in black silk or satin, she was endowed with an imposing stature
and prodigious stamina, frequently walking miles to attend her
Yorkshire engagements. She regularly walked to Leeds for her concert
engagements, covering some thirty miles for the return journey and
declared:

> as for walking to Huddersfield or Halifax to attend a practice, or fulfil
> an engagement, I thought no more of it than stepping across the stage.

For several years she walked from Brighouse every Sunday morning to sing in the choir at St Paul's Church, Huddersfield, returning home again on foot after evening worship, frequently soaked to the skin (Figure 6).[16]

Her final appearance as a principal at a quarterly concert of the Huddersfield Choral Society was in *Judas Maccabaeus* on 10 April 1863, the oratorio from which she had sung extracts at her début in Deighton thirty years earlier. However, when the chorus subsequently decided to enter the proposed national competition of choirs to be held at the Crystal Palace, Mrs Sunderland sang at a fundraising concert to cover the expenses of the trip. 'Occasionally', stated a report, 'there were symptoms of the weakening power of mature

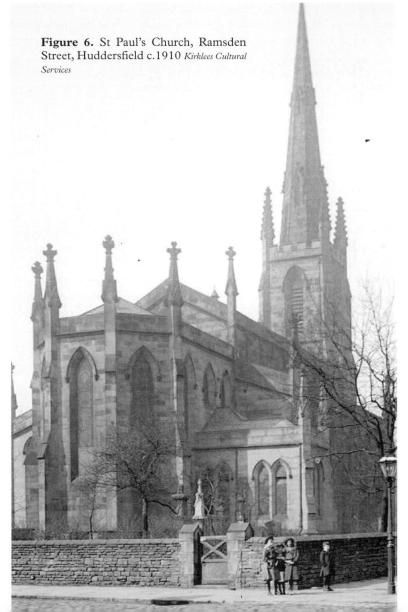

Figure 6. St Paul's Church, Ramsden Street, Huddersfield c.1910 *Kirklees Cultural Services*

years'. A surviving letter from Mrs Sunderland to Mr Brown, a Huddersfield printer, in March 1864 reveals her determination to retire at the end of the 1864 season after singing at concerts in Halifax, Leeds, Dewsbury, Bradford and Wakefield. She agreed to allow the gentlemen of Huddersfield to manage her final appearance at a farewell concert in Huddersfield for her devoted followers across the West Riding.[17]

In her prime, critics had admired the flexibility of her voice demonstrated most impressively in her moving rendition of Handel's 'I know that my redeemer liveth'. Moreover her appeal evidently transcended social barriers. In the year of her London début, she also sang at the Mechanics Institute at Belper in Derbyshire, performing several popular solos, duets and a glee. She often sang at the annual soirées of the Brighouse Mechanics Institute and at glee evenings in taverns and public houses. For over twenty years in succession she sang for a nominal fee every Christmas Day at Halifax for the benefit of the widows' and orphans' fund of the Order of Oddfellows, 'never missing a single engagement and never failing to materially augment the funds of the charity'.

She also assisted in a Palm Sunday service at Slaithwaite Parish Church featuring the singing of hymns by local children in 1850. Ben Turner (1863-1942), the labour politician, recalled in his autobiography, that such was her popularity that tickets for her concerts were raffled in the mill where his father worked. Her favourite song was 'I cannot mind my wheel, mother' by the Leeds composer, George Linley (1798-1865), but she also enjoyed singing some of the less well-known compositions by Sir Henry Bishop (1786-1855) including 'Bid me discourse and Come sweet melody.'[18]

She retired at the height of her popularity at the age of forty-five. The *Huddersfield Chronicle* reviewing her 'brilliant career as a public singer of nearly thirty years duration', declared that her career afforded 'an encouraging example to all aspiring singers' and was:

> *an illustration of the fact that intuitive musical ability and taste, if combined with an amiable disposition, and a practical desire to improve by attention, perseverance and study, will ultimately assert its superiority and triumph over all discouragement and difficulties.*

Notwithstanding her humble social background, her early employment in a textile mill, her lack of a formal musical education and her domestic responsibilities as a wife and mother of six children, three sons and three daughters, she emerged from the distinctive West Riding tradition of choral music to become an accomplished singer of

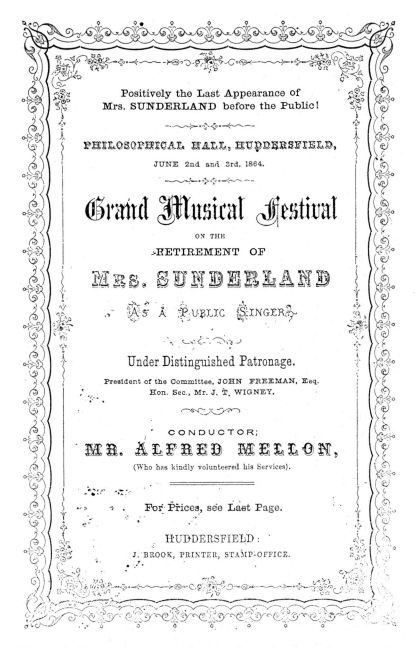

Figure 7. Concert programme for Mrs Sunderland's final concerts, 2,3 June 1864. *Huddersfield Choral Society*

oratorio and popular songs during the period 1834-64 in both London and the provinces. Indeed, musical commentators have speculated that had she been fully trained her career might have won her international acclaim. However, she neither sought nor achieved the international celebrity status of her contemporaries, Clara Novello (1818-1908), the distinguished English soprano, who had studied at the Paris Conservatoire and in Milan; Jenny Lind (1820-87), 'the Swedish Nightingale', who had studied in Stockholm and Thérèse Tietjens (1831-77), the celebrated German soprano, who had studied at Hamburg and Vienna and who judged Susan Sunderland's voice 'the finest English voice she had heard'.[19]

Her retirement evidently 'caused much regret in musical circles'. At her farewell concert in Huddersfield in June 1864, crowds unable to gain admission to the Philosophical Hall, listened outside open windows in the streets below and in the yard of the Ramsden Street Congregational Chapel (Figure 7). Large crowds later assembled at Brighouse Town Hall for her golden wedding celebration in 1888, when she was presented with an illuminated address and an exquisite, inscribed silver casket, plated with gold. A choir of about 112 singers, predominantly members of the Huddersfield Choral Society, conducted by John North were accompanied by a band led by John Bowling of Heckmondwike, which evidently did not succeed in playing in tune throughout the concert, which was organised by a special committee. It included in its members John Eagleton, secretary of the Huddersfield Choral Society.

Additional subscriptions collected on this occasion funded the establishment of the Mrs Sunderland Musical Festival, one of the earliest competitive musical festivals, which was administered initially by the governors of the Huddersfield Technical School and has been held annually in Huddersfield since 1889, except in 1940. The original idea had been for an annual Mrs Sunderland Prize to be awarded at the Royal Academy of Music or the Royal College of Music, but, after considerable discussion, it was decided to award prizes at an annual provincial musical festival in Huddersfield. Susan Sunderland personally attended the first festival at the Huddersfield Technical School on 12-13 April 1889, where a prize of five guineas was awarded, together with a silver medal for the encouragement of vocal music. The prize was to be awarded in alternate years to sopranos or contraltos and tenors or basses and the governors of the Technical School offered an additional prize of three guineas for piano and violin. Many singers who subsequently achieved national fame have been Sunderland medallists including Walter Widdop (1892-1949), the Norland tenor.[20]

After her retirement, Susan Sunderland engaged in private tuition and appears to have been persuaded to make at least one further public appearance, singing with the West Riding Choral Union, the Leeds Choral Society and the choirboys of Leeds Parish Church at a concert to mark the re-designation of the Batley Mechanics Institute as Batley Town Hall in 1874. Widowed in 1893, she attended her last concert, a performance of *Elijah*, at Brighouse on 15 November 1898. Three of her children pre-deceased her and she was cared for in her declining years by her granddaughter, Louie Sunderland. She died from a cerebral thrombosis at the age of eighty-six on Sunday 7 May 1905.

Following a service at her home and the cemetery chapel conducted by the Vicar of Brighouse, she was buried at Brighouse cemetery, where huge crowds, many of whom would have been too young to have heard her sing, assembled to witness the surviving members of her family, local dignitaries and the musical fraternity of Yorkshire pay its last respects to one of the county's most distinguished vocalists. Huddersfield representatives at her funeral included a former member of the St Paul's Church choir who had sung with her so many years before; Mr John Schofield, who had interviewed her in 1889; Mr John Shaw, President of the Huddersfield Philharmonic Society and the Huddersfield Choral Society and Mr B Stocks, President of the Mrs Sunderland Musical Competition, which continues to commemorate the association between the 'Yorkshire Queen of Song' and the town in which she had always maintained 'such a strong interest'(Figure 8).[21]

Figure 8. Funeral of Mrs Sunderland, Brighouse, May 1905. *Author's collection*

Acknowledgements

I would like to thank Mr Robert Edwards, Mr Richard Wood and the Huddersfield Choral Society for permission to reproduce concert programmes and illustrations from their collections held in the West Yorkshire Archive, Kirklees, and the Huddersfield Local Studies Library for their help in tracing illustrations.

Notes and References

1. This article is based upon research undertaken for the *New Dictionary of National Biography*, scheduled for publication in 2004, which will include, for the first time, an entry on Susan Sunderland. It draws extensively on the obituaries of Mrs Sunderland published in the *Halifax Guardian* on 13 May 1905 and the *Brighouse Echo* on 16 May 1905 and on J A Hargreaves, ' "The Calderdale Nightingale": Susan Sunderland, 1819-1905', *Transactions of the Halifax Antiquarian Society*, new series, volume 6, (1998), pp. 46-54.

2, J G Schofield, 'The Huddersfield Choral Society', *Magazine of Music*, June 1889, p.109 and type-script copy of interview with Mrs Sunderland, Huddersfield Local Studies Library. I am grateful to the staff of the Huddersfield Local Studies Library for helping me to locate source material for this article.

3. *Huddersfield Chronicle*, 4 June 1864; J H Turner, *History of Brighouse, Rastrick and Hipperholme*. (Bradford, 1893), p. 303; R A Edwards, *And the Glory. The Huddersfield Choral Society 1836-1986*, (Leeds, 1986), p.6.

4. Pigot and Co, *Commercial Directory of Durham Northumberland and Yorkshire*, (London, 1834), reprinted Michael Winton, 1994, p. 394; W White, *Directory of the Clothing Districts of Yorkshire*, 1853, reprinted, David & Charles, (Newton Abbot, 1969), pp. 547, 674.

5. Edwards, *And the Glory*, pp.5-6.

6. W Smith, *Old Yorkshire*, (London, 1890), p. 235; *Yorkshire Evening Post*, 29 March 1898; Pigot and Co., *National Commercial Directory, Durham, Northumberland, Yorkshire*, 1834, p. 260; *Magazine of Music*, June 1889, p.109; *Huddersfield Chronicle*, 4 June 1864. Some sources, for example Edwards, *And the Glory*, p.6, date Susan Sunderland's début as 'early 1834', but the *Yorkshire Evening Post* date of 1833 is based upon a programme held at the time of the interview by Mrs Sunderland and so may be presumed to be reliable.

7. D Russell, 'Music in Huddersfield, c1820-1914' in E A H Haigh, ed., *Huddersfield. A most hand-some town*, (Huddersfield, 1992), p. 661; Edwards, *And the Glory*, p. 6.

8. Edwards, *And the Glory*, p. 6.

9. Edwards, *And the Glory*, pp. 17, 20-21, 32-34.

10. Halifax Choral Society. *150th Anniversary Souvenir Brochure*, (Halifax 1967), p. 7; E Webster, 'Leisure and Pleasure in Nineteenth Century Halifax', *Transactions of the Halifax Antiquarian Society*, (1989), p. 33; Programme for the opening of Halifax Town Hall, Horsfall Turner Collection, Calderdale Central Library, Halifax.

11. Edwards, *And the Glory*, pp. 40-42; A.H. Robinson, 'Samuel Smith', *Bradford and Calderdale Chambers of Commerce Journal*, vol. 6 , no 5 , (October / November 1979), pp.9-11. I am grateful to Mr John C Jackson for drawing my attention to this article.

12. *Halifax Guardian*, 11 September 1858, 1 June 1860.

13. I wish to acknowledge the gracious permission of Her Majesty the Queen for the inclusion of this quotation from the unpublished journal of Queen Victoria from the Royal Archives at Windsor Castle.

14. *Halifax Guardian*, 9 June 1860; Edwards, *And the Glory*, pp.48-49.

15. Turner, *History of Brighouse*, p. 304; *Brighouse Echo*, 16 May 1905; Smith, Old Yorkshire, p.237.

16. *Yorkshire Evening Post*, 29 March 1898; Edwards, And the Glory, p. 49; Smith, *Old Yorkshire*, p.235.

17. *Magazine of Music*, June 1889, p.109; West Yorkshire Archives Service, Kirklees District Archives, letter from Mrs Sunderland to Mr Brown, Brighouse, 9 March 1864, KC 312 15/3.

18. Programme of concert at the Belper Mechanics Institute, 5 July 1842, Huddersfield Local Studies Library; *Magazine of Music*, June 1889, p. 109; West Yorkshire Archives Service, Kirklees District Archives, KDA, Hymns to be sung by children at Slaithwaite Parish Church, 24 March 1850, KC 200 5/21; B Turner, *About Myself*, (London, 1930), p. 24.

19. M Kennedy, *Concise Oxford Dictionary of Music*, (Oxford, 1980), p.635.

20. Smith, *Old Yorkshire*, p. 238; Edwards, *And the Glory*, p. 73; *Huddersfield Weekly Examiner*, 12 December 1970; J Sherrat in *Mrs Sunderland Musical Competition Centenary Year Syllabus*, 1989, p. 2.

21. P Edwards, ed., *From a Mere Hamlet*, Batley and Birstall Civic Society, 1975, p.9; *Yorkshire Post*, 11 May 1905; *Magazine of Music*, June 1889, p. 109; Brighouse and District Historical Society, *Brighouse 100 Years Ago*, (Brighouse, 1992), p. 42.

5. LEGENDS OF THE COLNE VALLEY

by John A Oldham

CUCKOOS, MOONRAKERS, LEADBOILERS AND LILIES are
the most unlikely inspirations behind the legends of the Colne Valley.
The valley is just over six miles long yet it boasts an industrial history,
which ranks among the most important in the world. It is difficult to
believe the claim that at one time a squirrel could jump from tree to
tree for the entire length of the valley. Even harder to believe is that
you could stand at a certain vantage-point and see over one hundred mills.

From the high Pennine moors that form the backdrop to the village
of Marsden the wide expansive valley drops eastward to the village of
Slaithwaite. The clear Pennine water races breathlessly over eight
hundred feet in less than three-quarters of a mile down the steeper
valley sides of the Golcar and Linthwaite areas before reaching the
suburbs of Huddersfield and its confluence with the River Holme
(Figure1).

The Marsden Cuckoo

Marsden is the most westerly village in the Colne Valley; it is also the last
village on the A62 before the road winds its way across the remote moors
and bids farewell to Yorkshire. Winter is hard on the edge of this bleak, yet
incredibly beautiful Pennine landscape and the celebration of the passing

Figure 1. The Colne Valley. *Kirklees Cultural Services*

of seasons has dominated life in these moorland villages. Omens that the long harsh winters are turning into spring still are eagerly sought, as the weak winter sun melts the last of the snow at the foot of the dry stone walls, and the insistent cries of the newly born lambs and the appearance of the crocuses, snowdrops and daffodils prove that spring is here. According to tradition the evocative sound of the first cuckoo is heard in the Colne Valley on 24 April at Marsden Spring Cattle Fair. It is this unlikely source which has provided Marsden with the inspiration for the Marsden Cuckoo legend of which there are a number of versions (Figure 2).

A cuckoo had taken up residence in a field and several people decided to capture the bird by adding an extra course to the wall. As they added stones to the existing wall the bird became frightened and flew away, just skimming the wall. This prompted the comment from one spectator 'Eh, by gum, one more course and we should 'a' catched it!'

The second version relates that the first cuckoo is heard at Scout, an area just south of Marsden. An inhabitant wanted to keep the cuckoo in the tree in which it lodged, so he set about building a walled structure around the tree. He had practically completed the task and was in the process of adding a roof when the bird took flight and made an escape.

Yet another version of the story tells us that a cuckoo had lodged itself in a chimney. An attempt was made to add some bricks to the chimney in order

Figure 2. The Marsden Cuckoo. *Kirklees Cultural Services*

Figure 3. Hare and Hounds, Hard End, Marsden. *Kirklees Cultural Services*

to prevent the bird from flying away. Surprise, surprise! The cuckoo managed to fly away before all the bricks could be added to the chimney!

The story of the attempted capture and 'letting out' of the cuckoo has been told, with various changes, in other villages. Apparently the village of Austwick in Yorkshire is credited with making the first attempt to capture the cuckoo. So the villagers of Marsden may have taken a story and adapted it so that it becomes, quite rightly, their own Marsden Cuckoo legend.

During the nineteenth century Marsden is reputed to have had the largest textile mill in the world. For this is textile country with mills that still make some of the finest worsted cloth. It was also Luddite country. General Maitland, the military genius brought in by the Government to quell the Luddite Rebellion, had no doubts as to where the heart of the problem lay - the Colne Valley. More troops were flooded into the area than Wellington had at his disposal in the Peninsular Wars.

Marsden found itself in the eye of the storm because local ironworkers, the Taylor Brothers, made the cropping frames that helped to spark the Rebellion. It was also a Marsden mill owner, William Horsfall, who was one of the first to use these hated frames and to die at the hands of the Luddites. Local people who worked in the textile cottage industry must have looked on aghast as more and more jobs were swept into the degrading drudgery of the mills. In the midst of this troubled history the legend of the Marsden Cuckoo shows a remarkable strength of character within the villagers to be able to laugh at themselves.

Slaithwaite Moonrakers

Smugglers at the time of the Napoleonic Wars, illicit whisky and gin stills, burglars, drunken lads trying to rake the moon out of the canal are just a few of the inspirations for the next legend set along the valley in Slaithwaite. The village name trips up TV and Radio announcers when they introduce the songs of Slaithwaite's most famous son, Haydn Wood (composer of many songs including 'Roses of Picardy'). The choice of pronunciation ranges from 'Slawit', 'Slafwaite' or 'Slaythwaite'. (One of the guards on the transpennine trains edged his bets by announcing all three pronunciations!) The village lies at the heart of the upper valley and is renowned for its magnificent mills, sixteenth century Slaithwaite Hall and 'Slawit Docks' on the Huddersfield Narrow Canal.

The canal rises three hundred feet through forty-two locks from Huddersfield before it enters Standedge Tunnel, the longest, highest and deepest canal tunnel in the country. The canal and docks are the main sources for our next legend, of which six different versions have been discovered.

One of the most popular versions of this story recalls the experience of some young men on their way home after having spent a night in the local hostelry. When they saw the reflection of the moon in the canal they thought it was a huge cheese floating in the water and tried to rake it out.

A variation of this recalls some young men, a little the worse for drink, staring at the 'face' of the moon in the canal. Convinced that it was a corpse floating in the water they were promptly sobered up by the experience. They rushed to the nearest farmhouse to borrow some rakes so they could rake the 'corpse' out of the canal.

Yet another version tells us about a group of young men who were watching the reflection of the moon in the canal and they noticed that it was moving towards a bridge. 'When it gets under t'bridge we'll get it aht', suggested one of them. They assembled themselves on the bridge and leaned over, each one catching the ankles of the next one to form a human chain. They nearly achieved their objective when one of them said, 'Just a minute till ah spit on me 'ands'.

A number of the Moonraker stories would appear to come from the early part of the nineteenth century at the time of the Napoleonic Wars when goods liable to excise duty passed along the canal. England was at war with France but apparently there was a large amount of smuggling wines and spirits into this country. These contraband goods would be brought up the canal to the docks and hidden in the canal. Under the cover of darkness the smugglers or their agents would retrieve them and sell them at discounted prices to willing local buyers. On one occasion the local constable interrupted them and when asked what they were doing, they pointed to the reflection of the moon in the canal and replied that they were raking the lump of cheese out of the canal.

Illicit whisky and gin stills must have provided a profitable sideline for inhabitants in the valley. One 'distiller', fearing a visit from the excise inspector hid a barrel of illicit spirit in the canal. When he thought the danger was over he decided one night to reclaim the illicit barrel. Unfortunately the excise inspector interrupted him. 'Nah then what ta doinn', asked the inspector. 'Ah'm nobbut trying t'rake mooin aht o't cut', came the reply.

The final version is a variation of the above story with a burglar hiding his loot in the canal. When he thought things had cooled down he went to retrieve the stolen goods only to be interrupted by the local constable. Upon being asked what he was doing, he replied that he was raking the moon out of the canal.

The story of the Slaithwaite Moonrakers is an example of a legend, similar to the Marsden Cuckoo, which circulated in another part of the country. In this case there are stories of Moonrakers to be found in Wiltshire. There were connections in the textile trade between Wiltshire and West Yorkshire, and it is feasible that they may have shared the same legends. Whatever the reason it does not demean the integrity of the legend of the Slaithwaite Moonrakers. Rather it enhances the reputation of a village that can laugh at itself, and cleverly turn the tables on those who choose to poke fun at them. It illustrates a gift for adapting and developing a legend within its own Community.

Legends from Linthwaite

A headless horsemen, the repair of a leaking tap and a secret passage are the most unlikely sources of legends from Linthwaite The village sprawls from the valley bottom, through clusters of hamlets and up the steep valley side to the commanding heights which overlooks its neighbour, Golcar. The nine-teenth century Ramsden Mill at Linthwaite was one of the earliest textile mills.

Linthwaite Hall, built in the seventeenth century, is the source of the two local legends. The first legend concerns an old chieftain who was considered a 'petty king' by the villagers. He was beheaded in a local field after committing an offence against the Crown. There is a report of a local man having seen the old chieftain watering his horse at a well near the hall one evening 'without his head', having 'come again' as 'The Headless Horseman of Linthwaite Old Hall' (Figure 4).

Figure 4. Linthwaite Hall. *Kirklees Cultural Services*

Ask any young person who lives within the vicinity of Linthwaite Hall about the second legend, and they will eagerly share with you the information they have concerning the 'Secret Passage', which links the Hall to Kitchen Fold. There are a number of secret passage stories, normally connected with castles, monasteries and old halls, which tell of passages built as a means of escape by prisoners, or when the occupants were under siege.

Our next legend from Linthwaite brings us to the late nineteenth century. By this time mechanisation of the textile industry had completed its stranglehold with scores of huge mills in the valley turning out material to clothe the empire. Millworkers would meet to drink and spend an evening in a small wooden or stone building called a 'cot'. The floor would have probably been constructed of compacted earth or stone flags, and the furniture would have been quite sparse with a few rough hewn chairs and tables. The pot from which they drank would have been metal, with a nick mark to show the measure of a pint. Heating would have very likely been an open-hearth fire with inadequate ventilation. They must have been pretty dismal places, smoke ridden, with the dimmest of light to be able to re-fill the pots. Barely a dozen men could have fitted into the smaller cots, yet they provided a meeting place and cheap ale. There were a number of these cots in the valley, some of which later became Working Men's Clubs.

On a typical evening one of the few men who was literate would read from the newspaper. This practice continued a tradition, which went back to the early part of the nineteenth century, when groups of Luddites would meet to listen avidly to reports from the *Leeds Mercury* of the disturbances in Nottingham. These reports would form a model for their campaign in the Colne Valley.

Although the *Leeds Mercury* had circulated in the district since 1717, a large number of stories and legends were passed on by the local equivalent of the travelling storyteller, the 'yarnspinner'. These yarnspinners would be guaranteed a free supply of ale for the evening to provide entertainment in the form of stories, legends, anecdotes and yarns. The use of the term yarnspinner may have been an example of local humorous play on words as this was also the name of a job in the mill.

Many of the legends of the Colne Valley would have been circulated by the yarnspinner who would dip into his vast repository of stories and legends. Like any entertainer or stand up comic he would have walked the thin line of humour that poked fun at his audience, yet recalling derogatory stories against other villages in the valley.

The cot at Linthwaite had the luxury of a tap that had become a source of considerable annoyance because it was leaking. After prolonged discussion someone came forward with the remarkable observation, 'Let's pay a visit t'riflers at Crosland Hill and get t'lead bullets. Wi can boil t'bullets in a pan o' watter and fix t'leak'.

The suggestion was obviously seized upon with relish, the visit to the rifler made and the bullets duly obtained. They prepared the pan of boiling water and expectations were high when the lead bullets were thrown into the pan, with someone testing them from time to time with a fork.

The legend records no details of the reaction of the members of the cot when it dawned on them that lead would never melt in water! We are left only with the celebrated remark of a local blacksmith who 'struck' a commemorative medal with the inscription, 'Hardly enough, John Thomas'.

A second medal was struck with a pint pot in the middle of a cross motif, with metal files forming the three sections of the cross. The latter was a reference, of course, to the Linthwaite cot practice of filing a nick inside a metal pot to indicate the pint measure. The A.S.P.F. and L.B.A presented the medal in commemoration of the Pot Filing Occasion. The cryptic letters referred to the 'Amalgamated Society of Pot Filers and Lead Boilers Associations' thus ensuring that ridicule would be poured on succeeding generations of 'Linfitters'.

The Golcar Lily
If you stand on the upper reaches of Linthwaite and look across the valley it is immediately obvious why the village of Golcar has been favourably likened to an Italian hill village and Sir John Betjamen called it the 'Provence of the North'. At the heart of the village is a tightly knit community of weavers' cottages, which defy gravity as they cling perilously to the steep hillside. A complex labyrinth of snickets and ginnels has grown

Figure 5. Golcar from Linthwaite. Kirklees Cultural Services

around these three storeyed cottages, with the workshop on the top storey and their characteristic long mullioned windows (Figure 5).

The click of sheep shears and the clatter of shuttles could be heard from the scattered hill farms and cottages since the early part of the fourteenth century. Despite its stunning yet inconvenient location, Golcar became the most important handloom weaving centre in the West Riding in the mid-nineteenth century. The village dominated the textile trade in the valley at this time as the Colne Valley Museum, which is housed in three weavers' cottages in the village, testifies. There was more than a hint of jealousy at the prominence of Golcar in the valley jibe, 'Golcar! That's weer everyone owns theer own house and one next to it.'

Watching the working demonstrations of spinning and weaving, an insight can be obtained, into the lives of these proud, independent and hard working Pennine hill people. They used their creative and imaginative gifts to supply their unique cloth to the world. Golcar typifies the two most important characteristics, which has helped to mould the communities in the valley - water and wool. The soft Pennine water that helped to process the wool and later to drive the factories. It also provided one of the numerous inspirations for the legend associated with the village, the Golcar Lily

A number of versions of this legend refer to the lilies that grew in the village. An abundance of water gave rise to a large number of underground streams, which provided the habitat for the Golcar Lily to flourish.

One of the most popular versions of this legend refers to the young ladies of Golcar, who to this day are called Golcar Lilies. This is attributed to the soft water and the hillside breezes that blow onto the village. These factors give the young ladies of the village a complexion, which is pink, fresh and handsome, just like the lily.

Lilies were reputed to grow near the railway station and on an embankment at Golcar. Another version tells us that a convolvulus plant with 'lily-like' flowers grew on a long high fence that ran adjacent to the railway.

The Golcar Lily legend has also been associated with the religious life of the village. In the early days of the village becoming a parish a large procession, headed by a brass band, would walk around the parish boundaries. The flag, which was carried in this procession, was reputed to carry a lily embroidered onto it.

There is also the story of John Wesley, the founder of Methodism, visiting the village who described the people of Golcar as lilies compared with the 'savages' he had met in the surrounding area.

When the successful Golcar football team in the 1920s travelled to their away matches, the wagon which carried the team was believed to have had the Golcar Lily painted on the front.

The last yet possibly the most enthralling version concerns the Protestant Huguenots who fled from persecution in France, some of whom may have settled in Golcar. Apparently they brought their weaving skills and the lily from their flag with them

Why do these legends prosper in the Colne Valley?
We all love to hear and tell a 'tall story'. Part of the fun in re-telling a legend is the 'naughty but nice' feeling of guilt that children (and adults!), feel when getting away with telling what we know is largely a fib. It makes us feel even better when the legend has acquired some respectability because it has become accepted as 'historical'. Within most of the legends of the Colne Valley there is a certain amount of 'leg-pulling'. The valley has had a peculiar genius for giving nicknames to individuals and to other villages. This is one of the ways in which villages cling onto their own identity. There is still a healthy streak of stubborn independence which unites the valley as a whole whilst maintaining the individual identities of each of the villages. Woe betides the young man who went courting a lady in another village. There are stories of these poor suitors being stoned away!

Rivalries between villages have been notorious. An early form of football game would be held between villages over two or three miles. It appears that it was more important a skill to be able to chop your opponent's legs away from them rather than score goals.

The physical geography of the valley itself has played no small part in shaping the character and distinct identity of the people who settled here. These are legends created by the communities who settled by the River Colne. Through these legends they have found a way of taking what is good and worthwhile from their past, of values that do not change and they have fed it with a humour which sustains them through adversity. It would be unfair to say that these communities live in the past since these legends still feed imaginations today in the form of the annual Slaithwaite Moonrakers Festival, the Marsden Cuckoo Walk and the Golcar Lily Trail (Figure 6).

It is not overstating the case to say that these legends help to make so many within the communities of the valley fulfilled, satisfied and interesting people. They have contributed a sense of purpose in their lives. These legends have also helped to create a genuine quality of life, which is still to be found in these tightly knit communities.

The stories that have been woven in this valley have as many intricate strands as those woven into the famous Colne Valley Cloth. They have been woven by such rich and diverse characters who have made their home in the Colne Valley for generations, and without knowing it have created a distinctive sense of belonging and their own special identity.

Figure 6. Moonraker's Festival, February 1991. *Huddersfield Examiner*

6. BRUCE OF HUDDERSFIELD: REVEREND ROBERT BRUCE MA

by Isobel Schofield

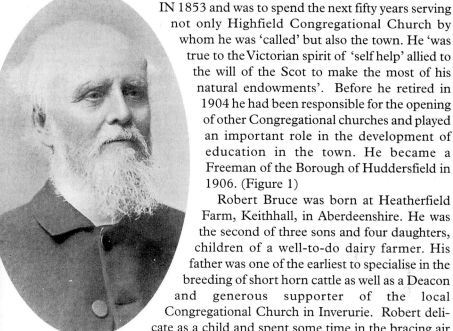

ROBERT BRUCE ARRIVED IN HUDDERSFIELD IN 1853 and was to spend the next fifty years serving not only Highfield Congregational Church by whom he was 'called' but also the town. He 'was true to the Victorian spirit of 'self help' allied to the will of the Scot to make the most of his natural endowments'. Before he retired in 1904 he had been responsible for the opening of other Congregational churches and played an important role in the development of education in the town. He became a Freeman of the Borough of Huddersfield in 1906. (Figure 1)

Robert Bruce was born at Heatherfield Farm, Keithhall, in Aberdeenshire. He was the second of three sons and four daughters, children of a well-to-do dairy farmer. His father was one of the earliest to specialise in the breeding of short horn cattle as well as a Deacon and generous supporter of the local Congregational Church in Inverurie. Robert delicate as a child and spent some time in the bracing air of Braemar. He went to Aberdeen Grammar school at fourteen before taking his place at King's College, University of Aberdeen. An enthusiastic student he was awarded the Simpson Prize for Mathematics in 1848.

Figure 1. Reverend Robert Bruce MA, DD. *Highfield St James URC*

After university Robert Bruce became a teacher of mathematics, first at a boarding school in Aberdeen and then at a similar establishment in Blackburn. It was in Blackburn that he acknowledged his call to the ministry. In 1850 he entered the Eastern Lancashire Independent College, which had moved from Blackburn to Manchester, later to become Northern College where ministers are trained today.

On 18 October 1853 Robert Bruce was invited to preach at Highfield Congregational Church. The congregation then invited him to preach for the first three Sundays in November before calling him to serve as their minister. The Church Meeting issued the call on 30 November 1853 but had to wait until 28 September 1854 when he was ordained and took up his ministry. He married Alice Briggs of Blackburn on 10 October 1854 and raised his family of two sons and three daughters in Huddersfield. For the next fifty years he and his newly wedded wife Alice served both the Church and the town.

Highfield Chapel

Between 1759 and 1770 Henry Venn was the vicar of Huddersfield. He was a friend of John Wesley and worked as part of the Evangelical Revival. When ill health meant that Venn had to leave the town his successor appointed by the Ramsden Estate manager was not an Evangelical. Unhappy with the teaching of Reverend Holcar Crook various groups set up their own congregations, the Quaker's Meeting House at Paddock in 1771, Highfield chapel in 1772 (Figure 2) and the Wesleyan Methodists at Old Bank in 1775. Highfield Chapel was rebuilt and enlarged in 1844 (Figure 3).

When Robert Bruce arrived in Huddersfield there were two main Congregational Churches in the town, Highfield and its daughter church at Ramsden Street opened in 1825. All other Congregational churches in the town result from the evangelical work of the members of these two churches.

Music and hymns are an important part of most church services.

Figure 2. The first Highfield Chapel with the first Sunday School. *West Yorkshire Archive Service, Kirklees*

Figure 3. Highfield Church. *West Yorkshire Archive Service, Kirklees*

Soon after his arrival in 1854 an organ was installed in 1854 at the cost of £850 built by Walker of London. Prior to that there had not been an organ so that the voluntary choir had been accompanied by a few stringed instruments. The choir was improved by the addition of a number of paid singers and the first organist appointed Abel Dean played for Church services for the next twenty-six years. In 1865 the organ was expanded as part of the redecoration and alterations to the church buildings. The Choir excursions were a special part of their year for example in 1888 members and friends of the Choir left Huddersfield to travel to Malham Tarn at 6.40 am, returning to the town at 10.15 pm, at the cost of 12/6d (62.5p). Paid singers were advertised for and auditioned and in a letter in the West Yorkshire

Archives, Kirklees, Agnes Sykes applied to become a member requesting a salary of £10 per annum.

Robert Bruce was known as a good preacher and lecturer and was one of the first ministers to give special addresses to children. He produced the first of a series of Church Books in 1858 that not only tell what has happened each year but give a historical background to the church and a great deal of information about the charitable work of the congregation. Not only was information given about the services, but also a long list of the various causes supported by the church and the amounts given by prominent members. The list of charities includes local educational establishments such as the British School on Outcote Bank, the Infant School on Spring Street as well as national schools such as Silcoates near Wakefield where the sons of ministers and missionaries were educated and Walthamstowe Schools for minister's daughters. Training colleges run by the Congregational Board of Education including Homerton College in London, Airedale College where fifteen students studied theology, and the Singapore Mission.

Religious groups were also supported by the Church such as the Home Missionary Society helping smaller churches in the West Riding. The Colonial Missionary Society working in the colonies; the Jewish Society founded to propagate the Gospel amongst Jews; the Port of Hull Society for the religious instruction of seamen; the Anti-Slavery Society, the Tract Society and the Bible Society. The wide range of interests covered included some that might now be considered as politically incorrect. Church members also supported a range of groups within the town ranging from the Huddersfield Infirmary, the Young Men's Christian Association, the Mechanics' Institution, the Temperance Society and the Female Institution.

During his time in Huddersfield the new Sunday School buildings were opened in 1864, an enlarged Manse in 1869, a new Congregational Church at Paddock in 1871 and the Great Northern Street Schools in 1888.

On only one occasion was Robert Bruce tempted to leave Highfield. He had preached at Queen Street Congregational Church in Wolverhampton on one occasion and firmly refused to do so again. In 1877 he unexpectedly received a call from the members of the church to come and serve as their minister. After much thought and prayer he declined and stayed in Huddersfield until his retirement in 1904.

During Robert Bruce's time in Huddersfield he was elected chairman of the Congregational Union in 1888. He represented the Congregational Church of Great Britain at the International Council of Congregationalists, held in Boston, Massachusetts in 1899. He was a Chairman of the Yorkshire Congregational Union, a Director of the London Missionary society, and President of the Huddersfield Free Churches Council. It therefore can be seen that he played an important role within the religious life of the Congregational Church at home and abroad.

He was also deeply interested in the town and served as a manager of the British Schools at Outcote Bank and Spring Street. He was the Honorary Secretary and a Governor of the old Huddersfield College, and very proud that the Prime Minister H H Asquith was an old boy. His two sons, Robert and Edward were educated at the Huddersfield College before going on to Aberdeen and London Universities. He was disappointed when the College closed and pleased when it was reopened by the School Board. Robert Bruce was an advocate of education for girls and involved in the opening of a Girls' College. He served on the School Board between 1883 to his resignation in September 1903. He became President and Vice President of the Association of School Boards for England and Wales as well as giving evidence to two Royal Commissions on elementary and secondary education. To further the cause of education Robert Bruce encouraged the movement for a free library and art gallery in the town, becoming a member of the Free Library and Art Gallery Committee. He was also a Trustee of the Huddersfield and Upper Agbrigg Savings Bank and a supporter of the Huddersfield Infirmary.

He was a vigorous advocate of the Liberation Society, whose intention was to separate the Church from the State. A Liberal, he and a number of influential members of his congregation were to play important roles in the development of the local government of the town; indeed several Mayors, Aldermen and Freemen of the Borough were numbered amongst them.

Influential Highfielders

In the nineteenth century members of Highfield Church played an important part in development and political life of the town including Huddersfield's first Mayor, Wright Mellor. Born in 1818 Wright Mellor was a member of Highfield for over fifty-one years, serving the church and Sunday Schools as a teacher, Secretary and Superintendent, and as a Deacon and Trustee. He laid the Foundation Stone for Paddock Sunday schools in December 1858. Wright Mellor became a West Riding Magistrate in 1863, a Justice of the Peace for Huddersfield in 1870, was Mayor of Huddersfield 1871-2, 1872-3, 1883-4 and 1886-7 before becoming an alderman of the first Municipal Council in 1868. He became a Freeman of the Borough in 1889 (Figure 4).

Thomas Denham, born 1818, admitted to the Church in 1840 was another who served the Sunday schools and was on the Town Council from 1868 and became Mayor

Figure 4. Wright Mellor, first mayor of Huddersfield.
Highfield St James URC

in 1868 (Figure 5). Huddersfield is largely indebted to Thomas Denham for his vision in the purchase of the Greenhead Estate to become Greenhead Park. His brother Joel Denham was another who served both the Church as a Deacon and teacher and on the Town Council before his death in 1883.

Frederick Crosland was Vice Superintendent and Secretary of the Sunday schools in the 1860s. A pioneer of the building society movement he was elected to the Borough Council and served on many committees, including the Huddersfield School Board, as President of the Young Men's Christian Association and as Assistant Secretary of the Huddersfield Mechanic's Institute in Northumberland Street. The Great Northern Street

Figure 5. Thomas Denham.
Highfield St James URC

Congregational Church grew out of his suggestion that a Sunday school be opened in the Beaumont Street Board School.

Alderman Joseph Byram was another who gave many years' service to the Sunday schools being Superintendent of the Girls' School for over twenty years. An advocate of the Temperance movement he was elected to the Town Council in 1868 and became an Alderman in 1871 (Figure 6).

Other important members include Alfred Sykes who was responsible for the two Industrial and Fine Art Exhibitions held by the Sunday Schools in 1882 and 1891. Joseph Woodhead was the editor of the *Huddersfield Examiner* for many years. Edwards Watkinson served both the church and town and was a member of the Board and for many years treasurer of the Huddersfield Infirmary.

Figure 6. Joseph Byram.
Highfield St James URC

During Robert Bruce's ministry at Highfield eight young men were called to the become ministers, the Reverend's Henry Edwards, James Haigh, Fred Moore, Fred Binns, David Smith Carlyle, Charles Shaw and Joseph Oddy. Between them they served as far afield at Sydney in Australia, Cape Colony, and more locally in Linthwaite, Durham, York and Birmingham.

Sunday Schools

A very important part of Robert Bruce's work concerned the Highfield Sunday Schools. Originally opened in 1811 the Trustees of

Highfield decided to erect a building at the west end of the Chapel House to house the growing school. 'The money shall be borrowed upon interest, to discharge which there shall be an annual collection in the chapel'. Built by Mr Joseph Denham the Sunday School opened in 1812 to offer education to the children who could not afford to pay for education. The teachers were paid and reading and writing ere an essential part of the curriculum, although religion played an important role. Passages of Scripture were learned by heart, 'apparently the privilege of joining the writing class was only accorded to those who evinced most diligence and progress in reading and committing to memory'. Children who attended other weekday schools, even those whose parents were members of the Church, could not attend the Sunday School.

The second School was built in 1843-4 when all the buildings at Highfield were renewed at the cost of over £6,000 (Figure 7). Opened in 1844 every pupil was given a new hymn book on entering the new school and many more could be taught. By the time Robert Bruce was inducted as minister the need for more senior classes had become imperative and extra rooms rented in the old Chapel House. The *Year Book* for 1858 shows that there were 260 boys, 255 girls with 72 teachers in the Sunday School and a Senior Class of 170 taught in the old Chapel House. A Library was provided, although it needed new books, and over 400 magazines were sold monthly. There was also a singing class for young people, presumably to act as a feeder to the Church choir. A Funeral Society, founded in 1840, to which pupils paid 2d (0.83p) a quarter for which £2 16 0d (£2.80) would be paid out on the death of any member. In conjunction with the Paddock Sunday school a Scholars Clothing Club was run to help ensure that suitable clothing was available for the young people.

Figure 7. The second Sunday School. *Highfield St James URC*

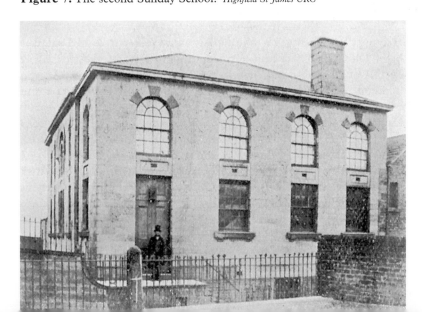

The Church also ran the Highfield Chapel Friendly Society, established in 1840 to help the sick, unable to work and funeral expenses. The society met once a year for tea on Easter Monday in the Highfield School Room. The Highfield Book Society encouraged the reading of first class literature with books changed fortnightly.

The Sunday School Jubilee Services were held in October 1861 led by Robert Bruce. Meetings and services were held over a period of three days. At the final meeting when thanks were expressed to the Ministers, organist, choir, ladies who had made the teas and the Decorative Committee, it was revealed that 1,940 people had taken tea over the three days, all who were or had been connected with the Sunday School. One speaker, Mr James Binns said

> *He never in his life did anything so reluctantly as when first he came to Highfield School. He had previously been accustomed to the birch rod as chief instrument of culture, and dreaded its administration. How agreeably disappointed he was on entering Highfield to find no such instrument of torture present. The good impression made upon him by the teachers of that time had never been effaced, and from that time to the present, he had been a constant attender at school, both as a scholar and teacher, either at Highfield or Paddock.*

By 1862 a meeting the teachers of the Sunday school resolved

> *that the time had come for the erection of new Schools, the present building being very imperfectly adapted for infants, youths and senior classes, and furnishing no rooms in which a gathering of the various sections of the School can conveniently take place, and being ill adapted for those numerous meetings for social and religious purposes which are so promotive of the interests alike of Church, Congregation and Schools, they confidently believe there will be a great propriety in the erection of handsome substantial and commodious Schools at Highfield as a Jubilee Memorial.*

Meetings followed and a foundation stone laid on Good Friday, 3 April 1863. The new building was designed by Messers. Paull & Aycliffe of Manchester. It included an Assembly Room, Lecture Room (for 200 persons), the Dorcas Room and several class rooms and infants room for 150 infants. The cost was anticipated to be £3,500 and was eventually opened on 30 October 1864 (Figure 8). A sixteen page pamphlet was printed about the service including Robert Bruce's sermon to be sold at the fund raising bazaar that was held on 11, 12 and 13 January 1865. Before the bazaar they estimated that they would make about £500 but according to the financial statement issued later they raised over £1187.

Figure 8. Highfield Sunday School, opened 1864. *Highfield St James URC*

Many activities were connected with the Sunday Schools including a Fine Art and Industry Exhibition in 1882 and again in 1891. During Reverend Bruce's pastorate the Young Men connected with Highfield Chapel started a series of lectures in 1866 held in the Assembly Room (Figure 9). A wide range of subjects were covered religious, literary, scientific, historic and of general interest. Such was the popularity of these lectures that by the Nineteenth Series they took place in the Town Hall (Figure 10).

Figure 9. Assembly Hall of Highfield Sunday School. *Highfield St James URC*

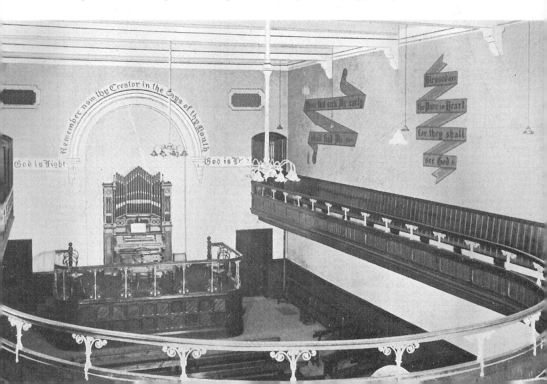

UNDER THE AUSPICES

OF THE

YOUNG MEN

CONNECTED WITH

Highfield Chapel, Huddersfield,

A SECOND COURSE OF

LECTURES

WILL BE DELIVERED IN THE

ASSEMBLY HALL

OF

HIGHFIELD SUNDAY SCHOOL.

1867.

I. *Nov.* 6.—REV. ENOCH MELLOR, M.A., of Halifax: "St. Paul: his Life and its Lessons."
Chairman, ROBERT SKILBECK, ESQ.

II. *Nov.* 19.—F. H. BOWMAN, Esq., F.R.A.S., F.G.S., of Halifax: "Books: their Use and Abuse."
Chairman, E. WATKINSON, Esq.

III. *Dec.* 3.—REV. G. W. CONDER, of Manchester; "Past and Present: or Steam the Civilizer."
Chairman, MAX. LIEBMANN, Esq.

IV. *Dec.* 17.—REV. JAMES M'CANN; L.L.D., F.G.S., President of the Huddersfield Literary and Scientific Society: "More Light."
Chairman, WRIGHT MELLOR, Esq., J.P.

1868.

V. *Jan.* 7.—READINGS AND MUSIC.
Chairman, Rev: R. BRUCE, M.A.

VI. *Jan.* 21.—REV. BRYAN DALE, M.A., of Halifax: "A Personal Visit to Vesuvius and Pompeii."
Chairman, JOEL DENHAM, Esq.

VII. *Feb.* 4.—REV. W. BRADEN, of Hillhouse: "Sir Walter Raleigh: A Hero of the Olden Time."
Chairman, ROBERT JACKSON, Esq.

VIII. *Feb.* 18.—REV. ROBERT BRUCE, M.A.: "Home, Sweet Home," with Musical Illustrations.
Chairman, WM. MALLINSON, Esq.

IX. *Mar.* 3.—REV. MARMADUKE MILLER: "The Teachings of Thomas Carlyle."
Chairman, DAVID SYKES, Esq.

The Lectures will commence at 7-30, precisely.

To defray expenses, the following Charges will be made. Single Lecture, 3d. and 1d. ; Season Tickets, 1s. 6d. and 6d. ; May be had of G. & J. Brook, Westgate, and at Highfield.

Figure 10. Highfield lectures. *West Yorkshire Archive Service, Kirklees*

Retirement

The *Centenary Souvenir of the Highfield Sunday Schools* includes a photograph of Robert Bruce and the Deacons in 1903, during his time at Highfield he had been helped by only fourteen Deacons, all men who gave great service to the Church and the town (Figure 11). A year later aged seventy-four he resigned. He wrote

> *Highfield was my first and has been my only choice and charge. Such a long happy pastorate is well nigh unique in the history of the churches. Most gratefully and humbly do I acknowledge the goodness of God in leading me to such an important and influential sphere of labour, and surrounding me during these many years with a loving, loyal and most generous people, who have supported me and my effort in religious, educational and philanthropic work with a heart zeal.*

On his retirement on 17 February 1904 he was presented with a cheque for £650 and an illuminated address (Figure 12). Mrs Bruce was presented with a diamond ring and tea tray by the lady members

Figure 11. Dr Bruce and the Deacons of Highfield Chapel, 1903. Including, Edward Watkinson (Secretary and Treasurer), Alfred Sykes, John Irving, Ben Mallinson, Abm Roberts, Charles Bentley, Henry Pearce, F W Dearden. *Highfield St James URC*

Figure 12. Illuminated Address from the members of Highfield to Dr Bruce on his retirement. *West Yorkshire Archive Service, Kirklees*

of the congregation. They moved to live in Harrogate where Mrs Bruce died in March 1906 with Robert Bruce surviving until 7 November 1908.

His life and death were widely reported in the *Examiner*. Following a funeral service in Harrogate his body was brought back to Huddersfield by train. A large crowd was waiting at the station and his coffin carried to the hearse by six Church Members all sons of Highfield Deacons. The procession to the church included seven carriages and the funeral attended by many of the town's dignitaries. The minister of Highfield, Reverend W Griffith Jenkins, assisted by Reverend D Forsyth, the Principal of Hackney College in London took the service and Reverend David Watkins of Leeds gave the address. Robert Bruce was buried in Edgerton Cemetery.

Huddersfield owes much to the life and work of Robert Bruce. The Congregational Church united with the Presbyterian Church to become the United Reformed Church. With St James's Presbyterian Church in close proximity it made sense for the two to unite and utilise one building. After much discussion and heart searching the two congregations chose the St James's building and became the home of Highfield St James United Reformed Church in 1978. The Highfield Church building was eventually converted to apartments. The Congregational Church in Paddock united with the Methodists in the Shared Church in Paddock and is part of the Highfield St James Group of Churches. Ramsden Street Chapel was demolished to become the site of Huddersfield Library and Art Gallery, Great Northern Street Church closed with many members transferring to Highfield. The large Sunday School buildings were no longer needed as education became freely available and were leased and eventually sold to the Huddersfield Technical College.

Sources

Dicks, J W, *An Inheritance of Faith*, 1972.
Huddersfield Daily Examiner
West Yorkshire Archives, Kirklees, Highfield records
The Centenary souvenir: an account of the origin and History of Highfield Sunday 1811-1911.
Congregationalist, June 1882
Church Books

7. EARLY DAYS IN THE MILLS

by Fred Wood

Born in 1913, Fred Wood spent much of his childhood in the Holmfirth area where his father was a tailor. In 1924 he left school and was asked by his father 'Are you coming with me, lad?' His reply to the question 'Will you pay me a wage' was 'I cannot afford'. A similar answer to 'Will you give my mother more housekeeping money' resulted in Fred refusing to follow in his fathers footsteps. Fred's story now continues in his own words.

I tried most painters and joiners up the valley without success and after a few weeks shed a few tears. Salvation came a few days later when a lady approached my mother and asked if I had got work. When my mother said 'no' the lady then told her that a winder was wanted at a small commission weaving place where she worked. I went to them and got the job (a girl's job) winding bobbins for the weavers (Figure 1). Of course I had to other jobs like going errands and emptying the rubbish cart which entailed me pushing the cart about 300 yards up

Figure 1. Winding Bobbins. *Kirklees Cultural Services*

Figure 2. Hollowgate looking over the Upperbridge to the main road. The building on the left was Parson's butchers and is now the Toll House Bookshop, Holmfirth. *Kirklees Cultural Services*

the path at the side of the river to the boiler house at the next mill. There were many of bales of wool stored in this mill and these bales jammed the river lower down at Lower Mills and caused the river to divert through the weaving shed and down Hollowgate in Holmfirth (Figure 2).

The weaving shed where I worked was cold in winter when weavers would wear their overcoats; the lighting was poor; toilets were down four flights of steps and across the yard. There were lighter moments when with the young men who worked there we would have an evening at Lockwood Swimming baths, six miles away. The tuner (foreman) always paid for me and I also remember being taken to watch Huddersfield Town in the midweek match when the lost in the FA cup with a last minute goal. I always remember that match because we had made little dollies of blue and white yarn and when they had lost in the midweek match I secretly took my dolly off, one of the lads saw that the dolly was missing and said 'We 'as thin dolly Fred ar ta ashamed that thi lost th' el noo'an allis loise tha wo's.'

With being around the looms I learned to weave and would often look on for lady weavers when they went down to the toilet and at slack periods the tuner would weave, and would say to me 'Will you take over Fred I have another job to do'. I always knew what was coming; it was always when the warp was nearly at its end. We called it 'downing', then I would have the dirty job of cleaning the loom, but the foreman tuner was quiet good he would show me a little bit of the tuning of a loom. Of course he showed me how to tie a cord on the bottom of the heald shaft because it was quite dirty, but I learned to increase the picking (sending the shuttle across) and also the checking of the shuttle coming into the box, if the shuttle bounced back it would leave staples in the cloth.

Our weaving shed was called Hobson Battye Ltd but was owned by a small bowlegged man called Smith, his office a mending room (two menders) and the warehouse was on Albion Street in Huddersfield. He would come to the weaving shed on Fridays with a cheque for the wages. I was bought a new bicycle for my fourteenth birthday so I had to go Holmfirth to the Midland Bank to cash the cheque. I did other errands, besides fish and chips I had to go into Holmfirth to a small shop that made meat and potato pies and had to borrow a butchers basket from a shop that is now Ashley Jackson's studio. I remember one errand to another small commission weaving place for a seventeen toothed bevelled wheel for the counter shaft - this language was foreign to me and I had to have it written down on a piece of paper.

The utility man was a called Fred Hellawell and did a bit of everything, weaving, warping, turning and twisting-in and healding. When it was time for me to learn twisting-in I had to sit in the loom with him as he did 7/8th of the job. He gave me a hook to tie round my middle I tried to twist with my left hand, he quickly told me to use my right hand. I said 'Why, I'm a lefty', his reply was 'Well you'r a righty now'. I also reached in for Fred when he was healding.

Figure 3. Victoria Street, Holmfirth. *Kirklees Cultural Services*

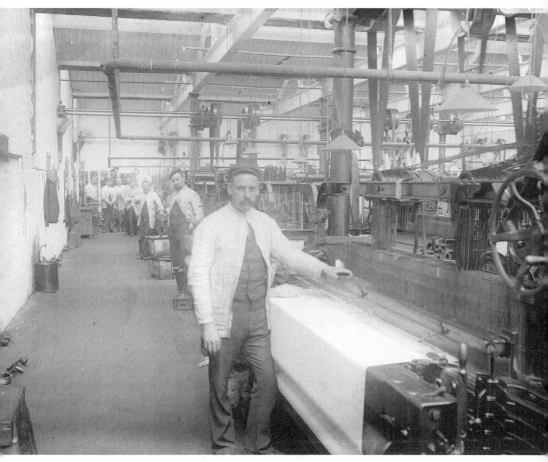

Figure 4. Dobcross Loom. *Kirklees Cultural Services*

Mr Smith the owner got fed up with commission work because it was the poor work that firms sent out so he began to make cloth for himself that were mainly good quality worsted and piece dyes usually white to be dyed to navy, brown or black. As time went on he decided that he would like the looms, the menders and office all together and bought a building at Damside at the bottom of Newsome Road, Huddersfield. In modern times looms would have been moved complete but being in the next to top storey of a five-storey building the looms had to be dismantled. It turned out that only six were needed, Mr Smith with an eye to business had bought six Bradford tappet looms that were faster than the Dobcross (Figure 4). The place at Damside was filthy and had been occupied by a man making boot and shoe polish. After giving most of the weavers the sack, no redundancy money in those days, not even holidays with pay, we eventually got organised. Then Mr Smith played his trump card – we had to weave two looms for the price of one.

The new premises were cold and damp and a small boiler for heating had been installed but it was never banked up at nights and was lit when a young man from the warehouse came in. Consequently the place did not get warm until midday, and then it would be left to go down. There was one morning when Mr Smith reviled me, we were working in our overcoats and he came from upstairs rubbing his hands and said 'Are you cold chaps'. He had just come from a tiny office with two electric fires burning.

I spent too much time talking to the two menders and my wage suffered, but approaching one Whitsuntide two of my friends with motor bikes said to me 'Can you get a girl for Whit Monday then we will go to Esholt (now Emmerdale) to the motor bike races'. I took one of the menders on my bike and what with courting and being married we spent the next sixty-six years together. I found that my bike had been leaking petrol and had to buy half a gallon of petrol for 6d. When we got back to Huddersfield I had to borrow the price of to go in the cinema from my girl friend and could not pay her back until the following Friday. I sold the bike I could not afford to run a bike and a girl friend.

I got fed up with weaving two looms for the price of one so I applied to the North British Rayon Company that had recently started up near home. My sister was working there and said they paid good money. I got a job working as second man behind the sizer. All that was done at that place was winding, warping and sizing. Yarn to wind came in parcels from Jedburgh in hanks and cakes. Artificial silk is man made, a solution is blown through a circle of metal with approximately 36 small holes in, inside a coagulating bath, in a mixture of many sulphuric acids which harden the yarn. The thin filament can easily be broken in the weaving so sizing has to be done. When the beaming takes place from the warping frame metal flanges are not used, but sheets of brown paper are inserted every few rounds. When the warp goes to the sizer the men at the back pull the sheets onto the floor but have to keep an eye on the warp in case a broken end has appeared and has caught on. Causing a round too many and holding the brown paper on to the beam (Figure 5).

The sizing machine is similar to a sturdy greenhouse with five cylinders inside made of Bakelite rods with a number of hot pipes underneath to dry the yarn. The yarn comes from the back warp

Figure 5. Sizing warp threads from the in-take end of the machine. *Kirklees Cultural Services*

between two rollers. One roller is immersed in a trough full of size, which is a gelatine or starch. The front man builds up the warp first with a sheet of brown paper then each edge of the warp runs a long piece of cardboard about 1½ inches wide with ½ inch of brown paper protruding. This carries on to the end of the warp until it is complete with cardboard flanges.

It was not long before I took over as front man, the older man that had been on front went to warp dressing. At that time I was working twelve hours per day, my pay was one shilling (5p) per hour, with no overtime pay, as the sizer had not to stop unnecessarily. I ate my sandwiches while the sizer was working and if I wanted to go to the toilet the old man would very reluctantly look on for me. At that time there was the Bordeaux system in which there was a card for every warp where the warper had to put the time setting in, the time warping and the time beaming likewise with sizing, the time tying in (a new warp to the old) and the time sizing.

The firm became very busy. I then stared working16 hours a day and weekends six until six pm. There was a time when the sizing machine was being overhauled that I started work at 11pm Sunday night and worked until 10 pm Monday night. This went on for seven weekends, that year I worked Christmas Day without extra pay. We had our emergencies, on one occasion on the late shift a young girl collapsed, with no ambulances available I carried the young lady down forty steps and waited for a motor car to come by. There were not many in those days but eventually we stopped one and took the young lady home. Another time when one of the men had been cutting yarn of a bobbin I went with him to Holmfirth and found a doctor that put three stitches in his arm.

The yarn came from a firm in Jedburgh and I often had to ask the old man to look after the sizer while I went to unload the wagon full of hanks and cakes for sizing. When the firm became busier I had to teach another young man to size. When I was working double shift I had to ask the manager for time off to go into Holmfirth to get my hair cut so after I had trained the young man we started to do shifts, six until six night and day but still working weekends. My back man devised a scheme whereby he would get into work for 6 am and check in for both of us. We would then speed the machine up but still put down the ordinary time on the Bordeaux card thus we were able to go home at 5 pm. I would have my tea, get washed and changed to go and catch the 6.40 bus to go courting and on my way go into the mill to check out both of us.

While I was on days there was an unfortunate accident. The manager, Mr Golding, came in and said in a brash manner 'Wood, go down the bottom there has been an accident, never mind the machine'. I went down to the ground floor, parts of the lift were scattered about and two me lay injured. An ambulance was called and it turned out that one of the victims was my mechanic friend and his labourer. I later got to know that while the mechanic was working on the lift that was stuck the manager looking over from above suggested moving the safety catch off. My friend did and the lift dropped to the

Figure 6. Sizing. *Kirklees Cultural Services*

bottom, my friend did not survive and his labourer, fed with cigarettes by the manager, never said who was to blame.

The firm got a new sizing machine with three big rollers (Figure 6). These rollers were heated from the inside and were placed on the ground floor as opposed to the old one on the top of five storeys. I was promoted to foreman on one shilling per hour (5p); the other men were on 11d. per hour. The manager, Mr Golding, came when the machine was fixed, he talked and talked and I wanted to get on with the work that was set for Saturday morning. He told me he was going to some friends in Nelson and would I send them a telegram reporting how the new machine was performing. I always thought this was to impress his friends, as he was going I raised my two arms and brought them down as a show of stiffness and agitation, he reached the door then turned and came back 'Did you raise two arms behind my back' 'No Mr Golding' 'Are you sure Wood' ' Yes Sir, I did not raise two arms' 'If I get to know that you did Wood, you are out.' I sent the telegram and he seemed friendly on the Monday. I knew Mr Golding was responsible for the death of my friend so I did not have much time for him.

As time went on I think the strain of the long hours got me down and one Monday when one of the office workers, the late Sidney Holmes, the son of the legendary Yorkshire cricketer Percy Holmes, came to get the amount of work that I had done the previous week, there was an argument which ended in fisticuffs and as a result we were both laid off for a week

Unfortunately I developed Rheumatic fever and was off work for about six months. Mr Golding took the opportunity to get rid of me and the Doctor told me to get a sitting down job working six hours a day. I saw an advertisement for a twister-in for night work. I applied and got the job although I was really as green as grass. My partner was called Sam and was a left handed twister; I was a right handed twister. Sam knew his job and we started each warp in the middle, sat on stools with the warp on the floor. Sam finished his half long before me, and I struggled with my hands stiff after my long illness. Within a week the palm of my hand and arm were swollen to the elbow. We started at 5pm and worked through till 6 am the following day. The day time man had heard of my plight and advised me 'Dip them i't jerry'. The day time 'Putter up' (Foreman) asked 'Do's ta smook' on receiving a negative answer he said 'Well tha wants to ar'an the thumb over bra'an paper it'll bra'an thee thumb'. I could never use a rubber cover for the thumb. I tried many times but it left my thumb icy cold and as oil and whitening is used in paste form it is impossible to use that medium and with a rubber thumb water and whitening has to be used. An occupational hazard was that thumbs were frequently cut so we used Friars Balsam, surgical spirit and in those early days a substitute obtainable from the chemist called Newskin. This was a hard glossy layer over the thumb, which made it grip the treads. In the early days, the twister in had what was called a hook tied around his middle but actually was a ring with a narrowing at the front where the knot from the old warp and one from the new warp was slipped through each other and slipped onto the hook (a knot being a bunch of threads.) To the uninitiated a twist is not a knot, neither are the ends glued together it is simply two threads or ends twisted with finger and thumb that holds together until the new warp is drawn to the front of the loom (Figure 7).

The firm did mostly contract work for the Government, e.g. railwaymen's and postmen's outer cloths, PEC's which meant privates great coats, RAF greatcoats and with many crossbred yarns for officers uniforms. There was one period when a piece of khaki greatcoat was fastened to four staves and half filled with water. It stood months and not a drop came through.

As there was not enough work for the twister-in through the night Sam and myself had a Dobcross loom each allocated for weaving when there was no twisting. The night weavers wove Northrop looms which

Figure 7. Pattern hand warping. *Kirklees Cultural Services*

had a round battery at one end that were filled with full bobbins by a Battery filler, this was over the box where the shuttle was constantly going in the process of weaving. The bobbins had a piece of metal around the top and as the bobbin became empty it exposed the metal, made contact with the feeders which were electrified. The empty bobbin was changed with a new one the old bobbin going through the bottomless shuttle in a tin holder. There were two weaving sheds at Washpit, one with Dobcross and Hodgson looms and the other where night work continued Dobcross whippicks, positive and negative looms Northrops, six tappet looms, four big Northrop for weaving Bedford cords and a number of warping machines and a winding frame. We night workers were the scum of the earth but we were only there because we had to earn money for our daily or nightly bread. We could not eat in the daytime canteen and were reduced to a small whitewashed room with no windows and an electric light bulb and a copper boiler to mash tea.

I became a jack of all trades and would stand in for anyone that was absent. I did battery filling, cone winding, wove Northrop for three weeks and even did a few weeks tuning. I was learning all the time. I must mention battery filling which meant pulling bobbins – when the full bobbin took the place of the empty bobbin there was always a bit of yarn left on the empty bobbin, the battery filler would empty the full tin from the loom in the alley and then turn the pile of empties round and round until the yarn on the empty bobbins tangled and he was able to pull most of the yarn off the bobbins. But as the floor was concrete the act of scooping the bobbin up resulted in the fingernails being worn down.

My work as a twister-in improved and I was eventually able to keep up with Sam although I often left blood on the twistings through cuts on my thumbs (Figure 8). I was earning more than the £2-17-6d I earned in my first week for 60 hours. One night I was careless while weaving a herringbone 8/8 piece and having two ends down healded them the wrong way making the cloth into a 10/6. I never spotted it when I went home and that day the boiler firer handed me my cars. I was overwrought, fancy being sacked from a night job. I should have got to bed but sacrificed bed to go and see the foreman. I had brought my cards with me hoping against hope, my first words were

'I'm sorry George, cannot I have my job back',
'No' he replied 'tha's made a mess of that piece, it'll cost firm payments',
'Please, please, George, please give me another chance'.
'No' He started to walk away and I actually pulled him back by his jacket.
'Please, please, please give me another chance'.
At last he sighed and said 'Alright but be warned that this is t'last taime'.
I was overjoyed and although I had missed my sleep I was still in employment. I started again that night and knew that I had grown up.

Figure 8. Twisting-in. *Kirklees Cultural Services*

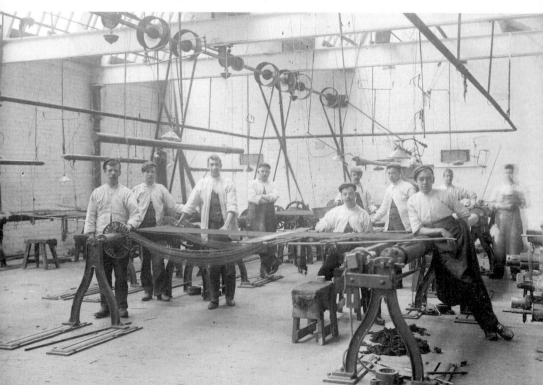

8. THE DIARY OF AN UNKNOWN

edited by Alan Whitworth

SOME YEARS AGO I WENT THROUGH A PHASE of collecting diaries. In a York postcard shop, now long since closed, I acquired a journal of mid-nineteenth century date compiled by the coachman to the widow of Mr J W Rowntree, the Quaker cocoa magnate. This formed the basis for my book, *Village Tales - The Story of Scalby and its Residents.* Another was given to me by a family friend, but it was at a postcard-cum-collector's fair in Huddersfield as I recall, that I bought for a small sum, two small pocket diaries dated 1923 and 1924.

The earlier pocket diary for the year 1923, bound in red cloth, is stamped on the cover, *Charles Letts's Diary,* and is published by the London firm of that name still in existence. It measures three and three-quarter inch by two and one quarter inch. The later, 1924 diary by the same company Letts, is entitled, *The Businessman's Diary* and is slighter larger and bound, according to an advert in the first diary, in blue 'Art Pluviusin Cloth Size four by two and three-quarter inches Price one shilling'. Both have a blind stamped motif on the cover reminiscent of the classic Art Nouveau decoration of the period.

Who wrote these diaries is not known, but in a small neat hand-written script, the pages are crammed with minute detail of the day to day life of a 'bachelor' resident in Huddersfield, and more, tell the story of his courtship to Edith Shaw, warts and all. The author, aged twenty-five, shares his thoughts and feelings for his first love and describes their outings, fall-outs and reconciliations in a beautiful style which could have been the model for Grosmith's *Diary of a Nobody.*

Yet while the identity of the author remains a mystery, there are nevertheless, clues to his social station. He was twenty-five years of age in 1924, which means that he was born in 1899, and an entry records his birthday as 30 July. This is also further confirmed by a piece of paper loosely inserted into the pages. The two diaries are like-wise inscribed inside the cover with the words 'Huddersfield 6 July 1985' in the same hand; was this the date when our diarist died and some relative or friend made a note here when the diaries came into their possession?

While initially the entries appear to suggest he lived alone, with no mention of parents or siblings, toward the very end of 1924 it becomes evident that he lives at home and there is talk of 'a Dad', and he records at one festive occasion, 'my folks were there'. It is also possible that the Herbert referred to throughout, and who married on 6 September 1924 and removed from Huddersfield to Paddock, is his brother, and that Winnie, who is obviously a small child, is a younger sister.

His occupation is perhaps easier to deduce. We know that he starts work around 4.00am in the morning and is finished by noon or there-abouts, and there is possibly a shop involved; and while everyone else is off on Bank Holidays, he works until eight in the morning. Adding these facts together, it has been suggested that a baker and bakery would fit such unsocial hours, as bread would be required holiday or not! That he was by trade a baker is also possibly indicated by his pres-ence at a local football match in 1923 - Sweeps v. Bakers - which attendance at, suggests that we are probably on the right track in this.

Such tantalising glimpses, but not enough to name him, nor place his address, except that he was resident within the environs of Huddersfield.

The man chronicles his illness, pneumonia, brought on by 'getting wet through watching Princess Mary' which left him 'too near either Heaven or Hades' for his liking, and records his recovery, nursed by Edith, during which period our anonymous author falls deeply in love. He describes his friends Jack who may possibly be named Jack Wilkinson (see entry dated 16 May 1924) and Ida, walks with Herbert and Wilf, visits to the numerous Picture Houses and Theatres of Huddersfield, sometimes three and four times weekly; Saturday excursions to Leeds Road to watch Huddersfield Town FC, and in summer months, to various local cricket matches in which Jack often took part. In all a wealth of miscellaneous detail, which, while we have no idea who penned the diaries, nor who the majority of main char-acters are, are nevertheless an important record of an age which is seldom written down by the 'common man' in so much detail - and for that, is worthy of a place in the annals of posterity irrespective of its anonymity as a fascinating historical insight into the customs, manners and activities of the times.

Finally, a note on the entries. In both diaries the writer conveniently begins with an introduction of sorts, which makes my task as editor easier, these are transcribed verbatim, but it is clear that they are written in retrospect and that some of the day to day entries are also, possibly he filled it in on a weekly basis. Apart from the introductions, the other entries, in nearly all cases I have transcribed these as written, without alteration, as the handwriting is in the most clear. In only a few instances have I had to add punctuation. Occasionally I have added words in square brackets to clarify a phrase or make a meaning more clear, and following the date at the beginning of the entry, in some instances I have added a note on the date as described in the diary, *ie* Easter Monday, Bank Holiday, etc. which note adds an insight into the entry, otherwise, all is as the author wrote it over seventy-five years ago.

1923

I write this on Monday January 22, as I find that the space allotted for that date is full. I have been sitting all alone with my thoughts and naturally they have travelled back; as far as Christmas Eve 1922. How I thank my old Pal Jack for all that he did for me that night, how he took pity on me in my loneliness and befriended me; no my mind went further back than I said, I forget the date, but it went to that night of the *Sorcerer*. How I felt that night, no-one will ever know; but to come back to Christmas Eve. When we had got back from Lindley and I sat on that couch with Edith, well how I controlled my feelings I will never know, but I was not then free to do as I would have liked, but gee it was hard to resist.

Monday 1 January [New Year's Day] - I start the New Year a bachelor, but dare I do what I anticipate?

Wednesday 3 January - I give Jack a great surprise as he makes his way to Ida's. Yes, he promises to help me and wishes me much luck; good old Jack. Edith is also surprised when I state my case what action will she take? Again I am left to wonder.

Sunday 7 January - Jack pays me a visit in the early afternoon. He gives me good news and I carry out his instructions. It rains.

Monday 8 January - Feel as though I could jump over the moon.

Friday 12 January - A day to remember. M[ilns] B[ridge] W[hist] Drive. I felt so timid and shy at first, but I enjoyed it.

Saturday 13 January - Met Edith at 6.30pm, had a walk round and then to Grand [Theatre][1] with Jack and Ida; I was awfully quiet but was too happy to ever speak. I did have a great time. Again I wonder, am I winning?

Monday 15 January - Hipperdrome [Theatre][2] with Herbert (Figure 1). Met Edith after Tec[hnical College] and walked home with her. I would have liked to have made love to her, but just dare not.

Friday 19 January - Mended a pair of boots and got wet through.

Saturday 20 January - Leeds Road [Football Ground] (as usual).

Figure 1. The Hippodrome Theatre. *Kirklees Cultural Services*

Met Jack at five and went to Banisters to tea.[3] Met Ida and Edith at 5.30pm then to Cowcliffe, a very good concert, a real fine time. Wasn't I just happy. I may be a bit conceited but I believe the tide has turned my way and I am winning.

Wednesday 24 January - Heeled a pair of boots. Met Edith at 6.45pm [went] to Premier [cinema],[4] had a grand time.

Thursday 25 January - Rotten day (£1 12s 0d). Income Tax papers delivered.

Saturday 27 January - Leeds Road [Football Ground] to see Sunderland. Met Edith at 6.30pm, then to Premier [cinema], then had a walk around. Had a good time. I learned that Jack and Ida had both been ill. Gee I used to think I was happy, but ye gods I couldn't have been. Dear old doll, the more I see her the more I want to and the more I like her.

Sunday 28 January - Jack came down in the morning, I was still in bed. Had a walk with Edith in the evening; but I do not wish to enter here what I learned that night, poor Ida, she must have felt awful.

Monday 29 January - I receive a bit of a shock, Lewis tells me he has given up Flo. Will he ever settle? I spring a surprise on Edith by getting on the same [tram]car.

Friday 2 February - I can't get my mind away from Lewis. I wonder what he feels?

Saturday 3 February - [Huddersfield] Town v. Millwall 0-0. Met Jack at six then went to Slaithwaite. A good show. Had a fine time. It rained. Another week gone; yes oh yes, I feel happy enough.

Sunday 4 February - Went in the wood with Jack. Dad and Win in morning. Took some fine photographs. Had a jolly walk with Edith in [the] evening.

Monday 5 February - Went to Palace [Theatre]⁵ [with] Lewis and Herbert. Met Edith at nine and walked home.

Wednesday 7 February - [Huddersfield] Town beat Millwall 3-0. Edith gone to a dance. I do hope she has a good time. She really deserves one.

Saturday 10 February - [Huddersfield] Town beat Sheffield 2-1. Grand [Theatre] in the evening [at 6.15pm]. Had a walk round. I wish one of two things; either that Edith could read my thoughts, or that I could speak them.

Monday 12 February - Raining again. Had a sleep in the afternoon. Picturedrome⁶ with Herbert. Met Edith at nine and walked [her] home.

Wednesday 14 February - Met Edith at 6.30pm, went to Empire [Theatre];⁷ I did feel so happy. The weather was dull, but I didn't feel one bit that way.

Saturday 17 February - Went to Berry Brow. Jack played, they lost 5-0. Met Edith 6.30pm, went to Premier [cinema] and then had a walk. I went to Jack's to tea. Had a good day. Was I right in my argument re fascination and love? I am beginning to wonder.

Sunday 18 February - A real winter's day, snowing all day long. Never went out until evening. Met Edith at 7.30pm and she took me in. It was fine to be there, with all my pals of childhood.

Thursday 22 February - It is now 4.10am. I have just got to work

Figure 2. Supporters and trams outside Huddersfield Town Football Ground. *Kirklees Cultural Services*

and on my way I have had Bull's Eyes shined on me three times.[8] Something unusual to see a P[olice] C[onstable].

Saturday 24 February - Went to Leeds Road [Football Ground]. [Huddersfield] Town v. Bolton [Wanderers] 1-1. George, Harry and Norman came (Figure 2). Met Edith at seven, was raining [so] went home with her; stayed until midnight. Had a fine time. Jack and Ida [?]. Everything points to me as though I am winning, but I do feel so happy.

Sunday 25 February - Took a few photographs in the morning and laughed until my sides ached. Met Edith at 7.30pm and had a delightful walk. I still feel doubtful as to what she really thinks.

Wednesday 28 February - Went to Bolton, [Huddersfield] Town lost 1-0. Nearly made a mess of myself; promised to meet Edith at six, [but] did not get home until 8.30pm. Went up to her [house], she was not very pleased.

Thursday 1 March - I must really start to be a good boy. Edith had a great deal of faith in me, but I must prove to her that I can be a man. Some fight.

Saturday 3 March - Leeds Road [Football Ground] with Jack and Herbert. Went up to Edith's at 6.30pm, stayed there until about eight, then went to Grand [Theatre] with Jack and Ida. A real fine evening. Well I really must class myself among the lucky ones, because after my behaviour of Wednesday, I was lucky not to loose all, even friendship; that would have been awful.

Sunday 4 March - Jack came down in the morning, I was still in bed. Met Edith at nine, walked home. Jack had dug his bike out again, I had to have a ride. A good evening.

Wednesday 7 March - Fartown to watch 'Old Boys' [Rugby]. Met Edith at 6.30pm, went to Grand [Theatre], saw Lewis there; I did feel happy, life is sweet.

Saturday 10 March - Went with Jack to tea, he went to Dewsbury. Met Edith at six; Edith and I to the Picture House and then had a walk.[9] I did enjoy myself, I was happy. It seems as though time has wings; it is always weekend and I just like to think that it will soon be Saturday.

Tuesday 13 March - Jack came down. We took camera to bits, then put it together and took some photographs.

Friday 16 March - A dull, cold, misty day. Jack called to see me, and asked me to go to Hipperdrome [Theatre]; something fresh to go out on a Friday. Mary transferred to Manchester.

Saturday 17 March - [Huddersfield] Town 2 Burnley 0. Went to Edith's at 6.30pm. Stayed there awhile then to Picture House. Walked home, had a fine time. It's a good old world is this and life is really worthwhile.

Sunday 18 March - Went up to Edith's in the afternoon, took a few photographs and stayed to tea. Baptist [Chapel] in the evening and a walk; a real fine Sunday.

Saturday 24 March - Leeds Road [Football Ground]. Met Jack at 6.30pm and went to meet Edith and Ida; then had half an hour at party, heard Hilda sing, then went to Palace [Theatre], fine show. Walked home, a really fine day. Edith thinks that my greatest interest in life is football; she is evidently no thought reader. I'd rather loose that than her.

Figure 3. Buxton Road with the Picturdrome on the right and Huddersfield Co-operative Society. *Kirklees Cultural Services*

Sunday 25 March - I should have been at Edith's at 5.30pm, but wasn't; got there about six. Went up to Eva's and then had a walk, quite enjoyed myself.

Monday 26 March - Picturedrome with Herbert (Figure 3). Then met Edith at nine and had a walk home. I shall be sorry when these Mondays end.

Thursday 29 March - Worked like a black all morning; something unusual, that's why I entered it here??

Friday 30 March [Good Friday] - Out with Jack [in] afternoon, and to Milnsbridge at night.

Sunday 1 April [Easter Day] - Sunday morning Jack, Lewis and self had a walk. Edith's at 7.30pm and had a jolly good walk round.

Monday 2 April [Bank Holiday] - It had to rain of course. Went to [football] match with Jack in the morning and to Leeds Road [Football Ground] with the girls and then to Edith's. Went to Grand [Theatre], a great day; Nellie and Ernest were there.

Saturday 7 April - Met Ernest at five and went to Cowcliffe. Had tea and then to the Church? operatta, it was fine, I enjoyed it. I took a few photographs. Life is certainly very sweet, and

Wednesday 11 April - Went to Grand [Theatre] with Edith; had a real wait in queue. Walked home, happy as possible.

Saturday 14 April - Leeds Road [Football Ground]. Went up to Edith's at eventime. Four of us went to town then to Hipperdrome [Theatre]. Hurt my wrist playing football, I'll never play again. Edith was, I think angry because I had played football; but I think she was also sorry that my arm hurt.

Monday 16 April - Met Edith after Tec[hnical College] and walked home (Figure 4). These walks will soon end and I shan't like that at all.

Saturday 21 April - Went to Cowcliffe and then to Brighouse with Nellie and Ernie. Had a real fine time, just managed to catch last [tram]car home. It's rather singular that Edith should strike up a friendship with a girl like Nellie, both are the type that appeal to me.

Sunday 22 April - Went up to Edith's at 5.45pm and then to Chapel, getting quite a good boy again. Then had a walk and I did so enjoy it, but weekends do seem short nowadays.

Friday 27 April - About like Thursday; oh no, I went to Town in the afternoon [and] I saw a dog fight.

Saturday 28 April - Leeds Road [Football Ground] for the last time this season. Went up to Edith's at 6.30pm and ye gods it rained. Went to Premier [cinema] and back home. I was happy in spite of the rain. Football as far as I am concerned has finished for this season; perhaps

Figure 4. Huddersfield Technical College. *Kirklees Cultural Services*

I may be able to prove now that I have other interests. I wonder?

Wednesday 2 May - Took a few photographs. Almost too hot for anything. Had a walk with Edith in the evening and came home with Jack.

Saturday 5 May - Went to Edith's about three, then to Almondbury. Don't think I ever laughed as much in one day before; but it did rain. Took a few photographs. I used be a flirt and thought they were happy days, but they were nothing like these.

Sunday 6 May - Went up to Edith's about 5.45pm. Fire cars there, had a ride to Dewsbury and back, then Edith and I had a walk; oh it was great.

Tuesday 8 May - Met Edith at nine and walked home; lost Monday's but gained Tuesday's.

Saturday 12 May - Edith a lot better, had a walk and then Hipperdrome [Theatre] 2nd House. Walked home, quite nice. HAPPY AS THE DAY IS LONG.

Saturday 19 May - Had a sleep in the afternoon. Went to Edith's in the evening, then went to Premier [cinema]. Edith had her aching tooth drawn; it knocked her over a bit.

Sunday 20 May [Whitsuntide] - Hung about the house until evening then went to the Baptist. It rained so went to Edith's and had music and fun. Edith a little bit shaky.

Monday 21 May [Whit Monday, Bank Holiday] - Worked until 8.30am. Went to Edith's at two and then to Brighouse to meet Ernest and Nellie, then to Sunny Vale [Fun Fair]. Ida won a doll. Edith pretty bad.

Tuesday 22 May - Worked until dinnertime and went up to Edith's about three, found her absolutely beat. Played table tennis all evening and had real fun.

Wednesday 23 May - Back to everyday life again. had a sleep in the afternoon. Found Edith a lot better in the evening. Ida hurt her leg.

Saturday 26 May - Hipperdrome [Theatre] 2nd House. A good show, walked home and really enjoyed myself. In spite of the vile weather and Edith being ill, I had a very good Whitsun. Edith stuck it well and she has a little bit of pluck.

Saturday 2 June - Lockwood to watch Jack play [cricket?] Theatre at night, met Lewis and Herbert and walked home with them. Summer came upon us today. I only wish I could think that Edith feels towards me as I do to her; sometimes I do and other [times] I have my doubts.

Saturday 9 June - Should have gone to Garden Party but the weather said no. Nellie and Ernie at Edith's. Played table tennis and I think I laughed as I had never done before. Some party. The best thing I ever did in my life, was done on January 3, 1923.

Tuesday 12 June - Met Edith at 8.30pm and went to Grand [Theatre] to see *The Flirt* and came home by [tram]car. Came down with Jack and a nice chat, quite a good time.

Saturday 16 June - Went to Cowcliffe to tea, then to Gala. Tried to dance, had a real fine evening [in the] Chair Contest. Nellie taken ill. Went into Edith's about 11.30pm, there was a house full, had a bit of real fun. If ever I loved a girl it is now. She is just my type.

Sunday 17 June - Went to Edith's at 2.30pm. Baptist Anniversary at night, a real fine service; Mr Potter in his sermon was great; then had a walk. A really good day.

Wednesday 20 June - Had a walk into Beaumont Park (Figure 5) [and] Butternab Wood with Edith. Quite a summer's evening and so nice.

Saturday 23 June - Went to Almondbury with Jack, he was not playing. Met Edith at 6.30pm stayed home until nine, then had a walk and came home about 10.30pm, had a talk with Jack and Ida and then said good night; came home with Jack. Summer has come and ye gods isn't it warm?

Sunday 24 June - Had a good time at Alice's. Paddock Con[gregational Church?] Anniversary, Lewis, Herbert, Edith, Hilda and Edith and I; talk about noise, we made some.

Saturday 30 June - Went to Belle Vue with Nellie and Ernest; tried to rain but failed. Had a real fine time and took a few photographs.

Figure 5. The 'castle' and refreshment rooms, Beaumont Park, 1891. *Kirklees Cultural Services*

Had a lovely hour rowing. Got home about 11.30pm. A great day. I don't think I ever go out now but that I enjoy myself.

Sunday 1 July - Went to Edith's about 2.00pm, everybody out until teatime then only three girls and me, I didn't think I had so much pluck; then went to Chapel and then a walk. Oh yes, I enjoyed it ever so much.

Tuesday 3 July - Edith's last day at Tec[hnical College]. Won't it be strange not to see her on a Tuesday. Still she will soon be starting again.

Wednesday 4 July - Went up to Barry to photograph a cake. Stayed there all evening. Had a bit of fun.

Saturday 7 July - Stayed at home until teatime, went up to Edith's. Had a terrible thunderstorm, Edith was ever so afraid, then had a walk. I only wish that I had known three years ago what I know now.

Sunday 8 July - Crosland Moor Sing, went with Jack, Ida and Edith. Edith comes home to tea with me and rain at night, we even go as a party, but had a real fine day.

Saturday 14 July - Went up to Edith's at 2.30pm, then went to Cowcliffe. Jack and Ida came up in the evening, we had a fine time; got home about eleven and then had a bit of fun and eventually got home about 12.30am. I am so sorry that Nellie should be as she is and I hope that she is soon alright.

Sunday 15 July - Baptist in the evening. H. Iredale and Hilda Shaw sing a duet, it was great. Then Edith and I had a walk. Then it rained, so had to come home, but had a good laugh when we got there.

Wednesday 18 July - Went to Premier [cinema] with Edith, hadn't been to the pictures for a month, a nice change; then had a walk. As usual very happy.

Saturday 21 July - Went to Cowcliffe after tea, had a fine evening. Ernie and I about as silly as we could be, had to rush for a [tram]car. Still it all adds to the fun. I wish everybody could feel as happy as I do.

Sunday 22 July - Went up to Edith's in the afternoon. Took Hilda's photograph in her uniform, Cousin Arthur there. Chapel in the evening, then had a walk.

Wednesday 25 July - Edith went to Cowcliffe in the afternoon. I met Ernest at night and we go up, had a fine walk; arrived home to find them all waiting to see photograph.

Thursday 26 July - Edith said something about marriage last night. I wonder if she meant it?

Saturday 28 July - Stayed at home until teatime then went up to Edith's, then went to Palace [Theatre] (Figure 6). It was 'Carnival Night', I never saw anything like it in a Music Hall before. Walked

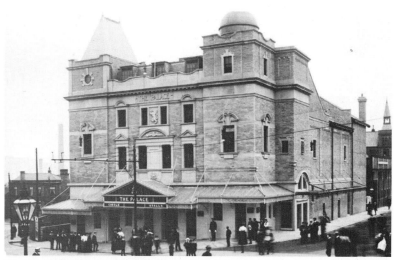

Figure 6. The Palace Theatre, Kirkgate. *Kirklees Cultural Services*

home, it was such a nice night.

Monday 30 July - I reach my twenty-fourth birthday. I get a card from Cousin Alice whose birthday is the same as mine, but I didn't send her one; I never think of these things.

Wednesday 1 August - Had a walk to Cowcliffe in the evening for some cloth. Nellie gone to Wakefield. Walked down the fields on our way back; quite a happy evening.

Thursday 2 August - Went to work for the first time on my one-pedalled cycle.

Saturday 4 August - Dora arrives about 5.45pm. I went up to Edith's something past seven, then she played the piano a bit; I tried to sing; then we had a jolly walk up towards the [? Paddock] Foot. I came home with Jack whom I had not seen for a whole week. If ever I had a pal, he is the one. He has done me more good than ever he thinks.

Sunday 5 August - Cowcliffe Sing. I had a good afternoon, the Sing was fine but I am half afraid to make an entry for what happened in the evening. I was a perfect beast.

Saturday 11 August - Nobody at [No.]163 only Edith when I arrived. Left there about eight and had a walk around Big Valley. I enjoy every walk I have with Edith. Again I must regard myself as being blest with good luck.

Sunday 12 August - Longwood Sing.[9] Nellie should have come, but she was ill, Gertie came. Quite a good Sing. Had a walk in the evening,

Figure 7. Longwood Stump, site of Longwood Sing. *Kirklees Cultural Services*

then a delightful hour in the room, no light, it was great (Figure 7).

Monday 14 August - Jack and I went to the [Fun] Fair and won a doll each.

Wednesday 15 August - Sweeps v. Bakers at Leeds Road [Football Ground], a real fine time. What fun, how I laughed. Came home by [tram]car and called at home for the doll.

Saturday 18 August - Leeds Road with Jack then to Co-op to tea, then up to Edith's. All four of us came to Town, but we left Jack and Ida and went to Hipperdrome [Theatre], a very good show. Walked home and was rather late. Edith got told off. Nothing ever seems to worry me now, I feel so contented with my lot and so happy.

Sunday 19 August - Park Sing, then to Chapel in the evening, then had a walk. Had to run into Gertie E.; she just about bores me now when ever I see her.

Saturday 25 August [Huddersfield] Town win first match [of the season] 1-0. Went to Grand [Theatre] with Edith and then home. I can't tell why but I felt exceptionally happy tonight. Jack got a duck in his last [cricket] match of the season. I wonder why Ernest is so narrow minded. Why doesn't he use discretion and commonsense; Nellie is ever such a nice girl.

Sunday 2 - Saturday 8 September - [Written across two full pages of the diary] - I spent the whole week in Llandudno [North Wales] with Edith, Jack and Ida. Need I say any more? The first real holiday I ever had and by far the best. Edith bought me an enlarger in Llandudno. How happy I was all the week.

Monday 10 September - How funny to have to rise at three and go to work.

Saturday 15 September - I witnessed the worst and dirtiest match I ever saw, but had come late. In the evening went to Premier [cinema] and saw a fine picture. As usual a happy time. I am getting quite used to my enlarger and find it doubly interesting because Edith bought it.

Saturday 22 September - Went up to Edith's about seven. Stayed there until 8.30pm then went to the [Fun] Fair. Walked home and had a very good time. Life just seems to be one joy followed by another.

Saturday 29 September - Edith busy making hats; went to Premier second half. Very cold, but happy despite that. I think winter has come upon us as it has been very cold lately; still, why worry.

Sunday 30 September - Doris went to Chapel with Edith and I. Harvest Services and very good. Then had a walk and yes, I love Edith more every time I see her. She is all that I desire.

Saturday 6 October - Leeds Road [Football Ground] as usual. Jack and I met the girls at six in Town, then to ?Dewsbury, had a fine old time there; but I was a bit tired and that's a new feeling. When I look back and think what might have been, well I thank my lucky stars and think fate is kind to some people.

Sunday 7 October - Took a few photographs, the three Shaws and at Cowcliffe. Had a good time at Cowcliffe. Missed the last [tram]car, got to Edith's just about eleven, still why worry. We are only young once?

Tuesday 23 October - Slaithwaite Operatta, Jack, Ida and Annie, Hilda and Edith making up there. Had a very enjoyable evening. Went to doctor's first of all.

Saturday 27 October - About the worst, rottenest Saturday I have had for many long months, didn't see Edith, but went to pictures with Herbert and I went to sleep. If last night was a taste of being a bachelor again, well I don't want any more, I didn't enjoy myself one little bit.

Saturday 3 November - Went to Premier [cinema] with Edith. Rained as we went home; didn't feel at all well, but was quite happy.

Monday 5 - Wednesday 7 November - [Written across entries] - In bed all these three days.

Saturday 10 November - Went up to Edith's in the evening, all appeared pleased that I was better. Went to Grand [Theatre] and had a very enjoyable walk home. All's well that ends well and last week had a very good ending.

Sunday 11 November - Went up to Edith's in the afternoon. We had a walk before tea then went to Chapel, and then had a walk. Oh I did feel to be in love tonight and I felt so happy.

Thursday 15 November - Got wet through watching Princess Mary.[10] Bought Edith a hair brush and comb.

Friday 16 November - I had to be brought home ill at 5.45am. I must have caught a cold waiting for Princess Mary.

Saturday 17 November - I have no recollection of what happened today. I know I felt awful.

Sunday 18 November - Tuesday 4 December - [Only one entry written across five pages] -Ill in bed.

Wednesday 5 December - I came downstairs to my tea, but oh I feel just awful and my legs just will not do as I want them to; if only I could get some fresh air.

Wednesday 19 December - If I wrap myself up well I may go out a little. Went to see Edith's father and called at Edith's; she was at home as her mother was ill. It did feel grand to be out.

Monday 24 December [Christmas Eve] - Edith came down in the evening; no she didn't, I fetched her. Spent the afternoon with Jack and went with him to tea. Had a full evening. Jack and Ida came about eleven, and I went up home with Edith in the early hours of [the] morning.

Tuesday 25 December [Christmas Day] - Had a good time at Edith's, and came home for seven.

Friday 28 December - Not yet fit to work so the doctor says?

Monday 31 December - And so the old year finishes with me still on the sick list.

Tuesday 1 January [1924] - I wish all my friends a Happy New Year. I feel it is my duty to make special mention of three of my Pals, namely Edith, Jack and Lewis, who have all stood by me during my illness, just like Pals. They have all proved that they are my friends in need, and a friend in need is a friend indeed.

1924

With all due respects to all my friends of past years, both sexes, I must confess that last year from January to November was the happiest year that I ever lived, I found love in that year, and if this should meet the eye of anyone who is afraid to love, let them take a word from me, it [is] the greatest gift that God gave to us, human beings. In November of last year I fell sick when I was in Llandudno [North Wales], a hand reader[11] told me that I should, but I laughed. That sickness was still with me, when the New Year came. But I learned a few things whilst I was down, and I believe that I am quite justified in saying that I think Edith does care a little bit, however, I don't want to be sick again to find out; no, I got too near to either Heaven or Hades, [and] I don't want to be so near again for a long time. But, however, I got better and working again, so all is well that ends well and my hope is that the coming year may be as bright as that past.

Tuesday 1 January [Stock Exchange Closed] - New Year's Day and I am still a member of Lloyd George's sick cabinet, but perhaps not for long now.

Friday 4 January - I go to see my doctor, he examines me and tells me that I am sound and able to work; thank goodness for that. He throws me off the Panel.

Saturday 5 January - I take a walk to Golcar in the afternoon and see Jack there, he wasn't playing football. Met Edith in Town at six and went to Cowcliffe, had a fine time there and saw a great concert. It was grand to be able to stay out.

Sunday 6 January - Had a walk with Edith in the afternoon and went to Chapel at night; then had a pleasant walk. I start work again at 5.30am in the morning.

Monday 7 January - It did feel strange to get up so early, but I shall get accustomed to it again?

Tuesday 8 January - Jack came to see me in the evening, had some music and plenty of noise.

Wednesday 9 January - Went to bed in the afternoon and then took Edith to [the] Premier [cinema?] in the evening. It was strange again to be out with her during the week.

Saturday 12 January - Went to Leeds Road [Football Ground] to see the 1st Round [of] the E. Cup. We beat Bramley 1-0. Went to Premier in the evening, had a good time and I am feeling like myself again - yes, I am fit for anything now. Alice and Clarence get married??

Sunday 13 January - Had a walk with the boys in the afternoon. Went to Edith's after tea, didn't go out again. Hilda sung us a few songs. I enjoyed that.

Saturday 19 January - Saw an awful display of football. [Huddersfield] Town beaten by Chelsea 1-0. When I got to Edith's in the evening it was raining so we all stayed in and had a real lively time.

Friday 1 February - Met Edith and Ida in Milnsbridge; had a talk with them, but I didn't feel at all well, and as I didn't want Edith to find out I didn't stay long.

Saturday 2 February - Went to Manchester with Jack, some trip, but [Huddersfield] Town won, but I think I shall be a long time before I go away again. I don't think I did myself any good going to Manchester. I felt a bit queer the day after.

Monday 4 February - Still feeling queer, perhaps it will work off. I have a sleep in the afternoon after I have got a load of coals in. I never got up any more. Felt awful.

Thursday 7 February - Had to call the doctor in, he tells me that I have got pneumonia. I wonder where that came from?

Friday 8 February - Too awful to remember anything.

Saturday 9 February - Edith came in the evening; but that's about all I remember of this day. I was in a bad way.

Sunday 10 February - I am about at my worst now. Edith says she came in the evening, but I never saw her. Alice says she also came, but I knew nobody.

Monday 11 February - I start to mend and I must say I always mend quickly.

Wednesday 13 February - Edith came in the evening [and] I knew her this time. I am a lot better.

Saturday 16 February - I may get up today, but must stay in my room. It feels grand to be out of bed, but I feel awfully weak and my legs have gone to nothing. I might have had some attack of pneumonia, [but] it only attacked my left lung. I think that lung must be a little weak, I shall have to take care.

Sunday 17 February - Edith came down to tea. I went downstairs for the first time, felt grand but a little bit queer. Had quite a good time.

Wednesday 20 February - Edith sent me two scones. Yes, I may try [to go] out. I went up as far as Edith's, her mother was surprised to see me. I felt [?low], Edith was ill, she didn't come down.

Thursday 21 February - I took Winnie up as far as Mr Shaw's hut, then called at Edith's. Quite a pleasant afternoon.

Saturday 23 February - Had a walk in the afternoon with Jack and

Herbert. Edith went to [Huddersfield] Town Hall at night to hear Hilda sing.[12] How I wish that I had been there. She called when the concert was over.

Sunday 24 February - I promised to go up to Edith's, but the weather went against me. I was miserable. She came down in the evening, but was not pleased with me.

Monday 25 February - I write to Edith. I must get ?confession right off my chest. I also see her at dinnertime, but I couldn't say anything as Lewis was there.

Wednesday 27 February - I again see Edith at dinnertime and this time I am alone and walk her home. All's well that ends well. We are Pals.

Thursday 28 February - I go to see about going to Southport Convalescent [Home]. Will I have any luck?

Saturday 1 March - Went to Paddock to tea, then after to Edith's. Jack I learn is not well. Edith comes down home with me and we have a very good evening. If I go away, how will I stick it, not to see Edith for three whole weeks. This is my first test. I hope I come through.

Sunday 2 March - It snowed like the D[evil] all morning but I must go up to Edith's as I may be away three weeks. I went up; had a fine time, but had to come home for seven.

Monday 3 March - Went to see *Orphans of the Snow* alone at the Princess [cinema].[13]

Tuesday 4 March - Went to Town to do a bit of shopping. I am notified that I go away on Thursday.

Wednesday 5 March - Went up to Edith's in the afternoon, her father had gone to work. Edith comes down in the evening. George Kaye and his girl came, had a good evening; but I didn't like having to say goodbye to Edith for three week's.

Thursday 6 March - I leave Huddersfield at 10.45am for Southport. I hope that I find both health and strength there and that I come back and am able to give Edith the good time which I am sure she has earned during my long illness.

Friday 7 March - A glorious day. Explored Southport and found it very nice, if only the sea wasn't so far away. Had to see the doctor but that was a farce. Weighed myself - 9 stones.

Saturday 8 March - Another glorious day but very cold. Settled down alright, feel as though I have been here a long while. Spent the whole morning on the sands. It was very nice, but the wind did blow. Sent a few postcards. It's a long while since [I saw] Edith on Saturday. She's a dear girl. I love her so and I already confess her argument was right and it isn't for "someone else".

Sunday 9 March - Another glorious day and much warmer. Again spent the morning on the sands. Went to hear the band in the afternoon. To the [?FM] in the evening and so ends the first weekend.

Tuesday 11 March - I hope the weather lasts as long as I stay here. Had a walk on the pier - 2468 yards [long].

Thursday 27 March - Leave here (Southport) at 8.55am. Home 12.30pm. Went up to Edith's, stayed to tea. It was grand to see the old faces again. Had to come home for seven. Had a great send off at Southport.

Friday 28 March - Home again; did a bit of [photographic] enlargement. Saw doctor, and thrown off Panel. Went to [Huddersfield] Town and Milnsbridge.

Saturday 29 March - Started work at nine. Went for a walk with Herbert in the afternoon. Went to Edith's about 6.30pm then had a walk and went to Hipperdrome. This was the first time I had been out with her since February 3 and I did enjoy it. It was fine to feel her at my side again. Absence makes the heart grow fonder. How I love her.

Monday 31 March - Start work again at four o'clock [in the morning] and I hope to goodness that I can stick it this time. Pictures at night with Herbert and Lewis.

Thursday 3 April - Went to see M[ilns] B[ridge] Scouts give a display in the evening with Jack and Herbert, and a fine display it was. I quite enjoyed it.

Saturday 5 April - Almondbury with Jack in the afternoon. Got to Edith's about seven. Didn't go out, Annie in bed.

Monday 7 April - Annie taken to [Huddersfield] Infirmary.

Tuesday 8 April - Jack calls to see me, asks me if I will go to [the] Infirmary with Mrs S[haw]. I go, and find Annie about the same, she is very cheerful. Went to a concert in the evening with Edith, Jack and Ida. Had a fine time.

Thursday 10 April - Went up to see Mrs Shaw in the afternoon to see if any news of Annie, but things are as they were on Thursday.[14]

Friday 11 April - Annie operated on, quite a success, for which I am very pleased. Met Edith in Milnsbridge, had a good little time with her.

Sunday 13 April - A rotten day, but went to Dyson Shaw's to tea; took my camera, but didn't use it. I like Dyson, he is a really good fellow and quite a sport.

Monday 14 April - Hilda borrowed my case, took it up this afternoon. Find Edith at home washing. Had a little chat with her mother and then went into the cellar and had a bit of fun down there. Went to the Hipperdrome with Lewis this evening.

Wednesday 16 April - Went to Grand [Theatre] to see *Young Rajah*, a fine picture, then had a walk round. I felt ever so happy tonight, but then who could not when Edith is there? I admit I am in love, for the first time.

Friday 18 April [Good Friday] - I lay in bed until eleven, and then I did a few photographs. I go to Milnsbridge in the evening and meet Edith. I go up home with her, and then we have a walk, and believe me, that makes it into a good Friday.

Saturday 19 April - Went to Town in the evening for a tie and then had a walk and got home about ten. Edith went in, so I went and had some fun with Jack, who I am sorry to say had a swollen face; he does look ill too.

Sunday 20 April [Easter Sunday] - Had a walk to Greenhead Park in the afternoon, then to Chapel at night, then had a walk (Figure 8). Met Cousin Samuel and his wife. As usual a happy evening.

Monday 21 April [Bank Holiday] - Walked over the top to Diggle in the afternoon with Edith. Jack and Ida came back to tea and went to [Fun] Fair in the evening where we were all pretty lucky.

Tuesday 22 April - A rotten day for weather. Went to Edith's about three. Didn't go out at all, but in the evening we had the room to ourselves, so we were alright and how I felt every nerve tingle with love for her.

Figure 8. Greenhead Park. *Kirklees Cultural Services*

Saturday 26 April - Went to Cowcliffe to tea, then to ?operatta; a very good show. Missed last [tram]car home, a bit late, still I was happy so I didn't care. It rained nearly all day. I have had a very good week; seen Edith every day except Wednesday. I rather like it like that. If ever I was happy it is now, thanks to Edith.

Saturday 3 May - Went to Edith's about seven, met Gertie Porter at eight and we three and Jack and Ida went to Premier [cinema], then we all went to Edith's. Had a good time there and came home in the early morning, but I never feel tired when Edith's there. If ever a man, had a maid, I must plead guilty of being him.

Sunday 4 May - Went to Chapel in the morning. Ye gods how it rained. Ida and Jack baptized. Gertie and Edith come to tea, a real house full, I felt quite merry and gay, had a real fine time. It's a great thing to be alive and in love.

Monday 5 May - Had a stroll around the market in Milnsbridge, but didn't see what I was hoping to see.

Wednesday 7 May - A showery evening, but had a nice walk in spite of it. Edith made Winnie a very nice pram cover.

Sunday 11 May - Chapel in the morning. I am getting quite good. A wet day. Chapel in the evening. It came fine, so we had a nice walk and once again I was serious for a short while.

Monday 12 May - Did a bit of lime washing.[15] Getting domesticated.

Tuesday 13 May - A bit more lime washing and printed a few photographs.

Saturday 17 May - Went to Almondbury, they lost [at cricket?]. Had a fine walk to Netherton and Crosland in the evening, it was fine and I wasn't a bit tired. Had a good bit of fun when we got home. Jack had to have his leg pulled. It was a happy day for me, well, all days are.

Monday 19 May - Developed photographs I took yesterday. I am not quite so pleased with them as those I took last Thursday. They may print alright though. Raining again.

Wednesday 21 May - Premier [cinema] with Edith. Saw *Six Days*, a fine picture. Had a nice little walk, but how time flies on a Wednesday evening.

Friday 23 May - Had a sleep in the afternoon. Went to Longwood with Edith, Jack and Ida to listen in [to the wireless?]; it was alright. Got home sometime after eleven and Friday at that; still, the more I see her the more I want.

Sunday 25 May - Went to be fitted for my suit and had tea at Alice's. Chapel in the evening then had a walk. Met Nellie and Ernest at Big Valley. Quite a surprise.

Monday 26 May - Again we four go to listen in. I wish I had a [wireless] set. Monday and Friday courting, I wonder what people will think?

Wednesday 28 May - I must be in love???[17] Had a walk on the moors in the evening. It was very nice and warm. Enjoyed it better than going to the Pictures, although that's A1!

Friday 30 May - Went to Milnsbridge in the evening. Saw Edith and Ida. Had to borrow 4d.

Wednesday 4 June - Edith busy making hats; didn't go out at all. Had plenty of fun though.

Friday 6 June - Met Edith and Ida in [Milns] Bridge and as Edith had not been working we had a walk. It was a fine Friday, and I don't care what the old saying is, I enjoyed it. I always do.

Saturday 7 June - Went to Almondbury to watch Jack [play cricket?]; he came home to tea with me.[18] Went to Town, then all four went to the Palace [Theatre]; ye gods how it rained. Came home by [tram]car. I love Edith more every time I see her.

Sunday 8 June [Whitsuntide] - Like a child I had my new clothes on. Went to Greenhead Park in the afternoon. Didn't go to Chapel, but had a walk.

Monday 9 June [Whit Monday, Bank Holiday] - Worked until eight [in the morning]; went to bed until 12 noon. Went for a grand walk round Castle Hill in the evening. A great time.

Tuesday 10 June - Met Edith and Jack in Town at 12.30pm. Went to Harrogate and Knaresborough by charabanc. Had a fine time, and didn't I feel happy as we came back. I could have ridden for ever. A good ending to a good day.

Thursday 12 June - This Whitsun[tide] has been vastly different to last, Edith was ill then. I have enjoyed every hour of it. It's really surprising what a good girl can do for a man. Love is truly a great thing.

Saturday 14 June - Went to watch Paddock [play cricket?]. Up to Edith's about seven. Didn't go out until 9.30. I was in a very queer mood, and almost made a mess of my life; I shall have to be careful or results may be fatal. I certainly wasn't a gentleman, but I can't explain why this mood got me, but I wish it had never come. I can't afford to hurt Edith, I love her so.

Sunday 15 June - Didn't intent to go to Chapel this morning, but some unknown [force] led me there, and I'm glad I went. Went again at night and really enjoyed it. Then Edith and I had a walk; really different to last night, I was ever so happy.

Wednesday 18 June - Went to Dyson Shaw's in the evening, Edith played the piano a little. Had a fine time. It was a delightful walk along the canal side. Saw Jack, he was full of cold.

Thursday 19 June - Had a walk round Jubilee Fields in the afternoon; I was alone. it was very warm indeed.

Sunday 22 June - Went up to Edith's about three, took a few photographs. Went to Chapel in the evening, then had a walk to Beaumont Park. It was lovely.

Thursday 26 June - Did a bit of enlarging [of photographs]. Took my grey hat to clean. Nothing very exciting.

Friday 27 June - Went to Milnsbridge in the evening. Met Ida, had a long chat with her. Edith not there, worst luck.

Saturday 28 June - Went to watch Linthwaite and Golcar at Linthwaite. Ye gods it was cold. Went to Premier [cinema] in the evening with Edith; had a jolly good time. I felt as though I would have like to have said certain things, but its so funny, I didn't used to believe in engagements but now my thoughts keep turning to them and I find myself wishing that I had the pluck[19] to speak; why am I faint hearted?

Sunday 29 June - Did a bit of enlarging in the morning, then went up to Edith's. It rained, but we went to Paddock and had a good time, but had to hurry home as we were very late for Sunday and Ida [did] not like that to happen.

Monday 30 June - Saw Gertie and Nellie in the evening. Went for a walk with Lewis O'Metz and Herbert, not so bad considering.

Tuesday 1 July - Enlarged twenty-four photographs this evening, I believe a record for me. I keep thinking I will give up photography, but what would I do with my time? I must have a hobby.

Wednesday 2 July - Edith full of cold, had a walk on the moor to try and blow it away. It was a bit cold, but I think it did her good. I hope so at any rate.

Friday 4 July - Enlarged some photographs for Lewis O'Metz and took them up in the evening. A thunderstorm came on, otherwise I may have seen Edith, but didn't.

Sunday 6 July - Went up to Edith's in the afternoon, had a walk, then went to Chapel in the evening, then went by [tram]car to Lindley and walked home. Had a bit of fun when we got home. I had a feeling of perfect happiness today. I would that it had been warm enough to sit down as I did want a serious talk with Edith. But maybe I will be able to do so on Wednesday. I really must before we go away. I want her, I love her, she is my ideal.

Wednesday 9 July - A glorious day. Went up on the moors and lay down; I knew just what I wanted to say but I could not say it. It got to my throat and stuck there, but after a long while it came out and I made the most solemn and serious promise that I ever made; I asked her to be engaged. Have I any hope? I wonder what her answer will be? My future happiness rests on that answer. Edith do be kind to me, I love you.

Saturday 12 July - Didn't get washed until teatime. Went up to Edith's, then had a walk on to the moors. Edith made me the happiest man in England, she said "yes". How happy I was - and now I realise that I must be a man and play a man's part. I won't give her a chance to rue her bargain.

Wednesday 16 July - Annie taken to Crosland Moor. Edith and I had a walk in Beaumont Park (Figure 9). Had a very nice time.

Friday 18 July - Had a cycle ride round Big Valley in the evening with Herbert; it was grand to be awheel again.

Saturday 19 July - Had a sleep in the afternoon then went to Edith's about six. Walked down to Town and I bought Edith a ring. Then had a walk down the fields at Almondbury and there I put the ring on to Edith's finger and became officially engaged.

Sunday 20 July - Had a walk in the morning with Jack, he congratulated me on my engagement. Had a walk in the afternoon with Edith and Hilda. Went to Chapel at night. It rained so had to go home, but had a good time there. Life is now really worthwhile.

Wednesday 23 July - Went up to Edith's in the evening. Went to Premier [cinema], got wet through [and] had to borrow Fred's coat. Came home damp but happy.

Thursday 24 July - Took Fred his coat back; called at Edith's, found Fred busy pulling paper off room wall, set to and helped him. Had tea there and finished walls after tea; Edith was

Wednesday 30 July - Met Edith in Town. Went to Hipperdrome first house. Had a walk, saw Lewis. I was quite happy as this was my birthday. Annie gives the Shaw's a shock, I don't know what is going to happen as she wants to go back there. Poor Mr Shaw is at a loss what to do and Mrs Shaw is again unwell. Why should some people have so much worry? We are taught to believe that all things work together for good, but ye gods, at times it needs a lot of faith to believe it. We must hope for the best in spite of things.

Saturday 2 August - Went to Fartown [cricket?] with Jack and Herbert. Had tea there and went straight up to Edith's with Jack. Learnt that Annie had gone home. All four went to Almondbury Rush.[20] Had a fine old time. Won a few things. Eunice and her 'boy' there; got on quite well with him.

Sunday 3 August - Went up to Edith's about three. It rained, so didn't go out until Chapel time, went to the Clough with Mrs Shaw, a very nice service, then had a walk and very nice too.

Monday 4 August [Bank Holiday] - Pretty much like an ordinary

Figure 9. Beaumont Park, 1881. *Kirklees Cultural Services*

day until evening; but it's a while since I enjoyed a Monday like this. We had a fine time at Almondbury.

Tuesday 5 August - Did a few photographs for various people. I shall have to get that sign yet. It's a good hobby.

Wednesday 6 August - Annie dies at 6.50am. Went up to Edith's about seven. Had a walk, but a gloom seemed to be over everybody. It's hard lines at twenty-five years of age.

Thursday 7 August - Had a busy afternoon in my studio. Went to Fartown in the evening with Jack and Herbert.

Saturday 9 August - Went to Jack's to tea, then went up to [No.]163 together. Edith and I went to look at Annie's grave, then came home and did some photograph's. Went down to the [Fun] Fair with Jack and came home in the early hours of Sunday morning; but why worry we both went home quite sober.

Sunday 10 August - Went to Cowcliffe Sing, had a grand time there.[21] Just about caught the last [tram]car up. I didn't want to leave Edith a bit, but had to. I love her more each time I see her.

Monday 11 August - Cycled all round outskirts of [Huddersfield] Town looking for either a home or rooms for Herbert.

Thursday 14 August - Went to Milnsbridge in the afternoon on my cycle, had a puncture, the first I have had. Did a bit of enlarging [photographs].

Saturday 16 August - Rained all afternoon so didn't go out until evening when it cleared up, so Edith and I had a grand long walk and we got [to] talking about when I was ill, and I didn't think she cared as much then as she did. Poor old doll, she must have had as rough a passage as I had. Bless her, she is a darling.

Sunday 17 August - Raining again. The triplets and Jack and I all go up to Dyson [Shaw], so had a jolly good time. Rain can't make us uncomfortable. Hilda sang, that was worth getting wet for.

Monday 18 August - A wild day, something like November. Took a few things down to Herbert's new house.

Wednesday 20 August - Had a walk in the evening with Edith. It's getting quite near to our holiday now. It will be heaven to have her a whole week to myself.

Thursday 21 August - Pressed a few things and got my case ready for Saturday.

Friday 22 August - Went down to Milnsbridge with the boys, then up to Edith's for their cases. Mr Shaw has a bad [cold?]. I wonder, will he be fit to travel tomorrow; for his sake I hope so.

Saturday 23 August - Holidays. Yes, Mr Shaw is able to go. We leave Huddersfield at 9.40am and get to Blackpool at 12.45pm - and then starts our "unofficial honeymoon". We find our digs and generally settle down to a week of, well we shall have to wait and see.

Sunday 24 - Wednesday 27 August - If anyone ever spent a happier holiday in Blackpool, despite bad weather, than Edith and I did, well I would like to meet them.

Saturday 30 August - But alas, all good things must come to an end, and today we leave Blackpool for home and work; but if I live to be a very old man, I shall never forget, and I hardly think that Edith will, this last week. Everything went well and we seemed to know each other perfectly. I liked my first "unofficial honeymoon".

Sunday 31 August - Back to the old routine. I went up to Edith's about three then we went up home with Audrey. We went to Chapel and then had a walk, and if ever I loved Edith, it is now. I must save all I can and make her mine. She is my first aim in life and then a business.

Thursday 4 September - Everybody else packing up to go away. But whatever they may do they cannot have a better time than we had. I take Dad's case down to Town. Edith's mam and dad return from Blackpool.

Friday 5 September - All at home go away to London to Herbert's wedding and I am left alone, a bachelor. I go up to Edith's in the evening and so starts our second weeks holiday. Ida and Jack and Hilda all packing up.

Saturday 6 September - Herbert's wedding. I go to Alice's to dinner and to Leeds Road [Football Ground] with Lewis, then up to Edith's. We go for a walk as the evening is nice. I wonder how everybody is that got away; I am quite happy and content, because what I have had no one can take from me, I have loved Edith for months, but it grows each time I see her.

Sunday 7 September - Didn't wake up until 11.15am and was to go to Edith's to dinner. Hurried round and got there soon after twelve and spent the whole day there. It rained all day, still I was happy enough.

Monday 8 - Friday 12 September - I really cannot attempt to enter here all that took place between Monday and Saturday as my diary would not hold it - but it is quite enough to put that I saw Edith every day. That alone is happiness for me.

Saturday 13 September - And so ends our second holiday and the great return begins, everybody comes home. Edith comes down in the evening and we go for a walk. By the way, I ought to mention that during the week I won £1 for my "Happiness Snap".

Friday 19 September - Helped Herbert to fetch his belongings from

Huddersfield to Paddock - ye gods it was a job, and to make it worse, it rained like H[ell]. Jack helped me with the bed from Shaw's; finished about midnight.

Saturday 20 September - Went with Jack to Leeds Road [Football Ground] to see Blackburn [Rovers], an awful match. After tea Edith and I, and Herbert and Dora went to Hipperdrome. It was a very good show and I really enjoyed the evening. I wish I was in Herbert's state but not in his shoes. He is in a bit of a mess but hope he soon gets things alright. My prayer is that I may be able to give Edith a better start!

Saturday 27 September - Was to have gone to Leeds but changed my mind at the eleventh hour, which cheered Edith. Went to the Hipperdrome in the evening. Had a fine time. Jack went to Leeds with Arnold, but I dare not risk too much, I don't want to be ill again.

Tuesday 30 September - Edith starts going to [Huddersfield] Tec[hnical College], so I'll see her now on a Tuesday night. I wouldn't care if I saw her every night. I have an hour with her. It's only short, but it goes a long way.

Friday 3 October - Cycle breaks down, takes me until teatime to mend it. Then I went to bed until eight. Met Edith at 9.15pm, had a lovely walk home. She is a dear. I love her more every time I see her.

Saturday 4 October - Leeds Road [Football Ground] with the two Lewis's; a good game.[22] Went up to Edith's after tea then went to Hipperdrome. Jack starts playing football for the Baptist's, wish I could play but Edith is glad that I can't.

Sunday 5 October - Edith and I went to Frank's to tea. He is a proper lad, we did have fun. Walked home and really enjoyed the whole day.

Monday 6 October - Did some photographs for Mabel at the shop.

Friday 10 October - Helped Herbert to do a bit of flitting and then met Edith, but it rained so came home by [tram]car. Edith a little bit off colour.

Sunday 12 October - Ida, Edith, Jack and I went to Fanny's at Batley, had a jolly good time.

Wednesday 15 October - Had a night off, didn't go courting. Surely a strange Wednesday.

Saturday 18 October - Leeds Road [Football Ground]. Edith's about 6.30pm. Silly side out. Went to Premier [cinema]. Fanny here. Jack and Ida gone to Manchester. If only I could have photographed my feelings I would have won the 'Happiness' Competition.

Sunday 19 October - A nasty day. Had a bit of music at Edith's in the afternoon. Chapel in the evening, then Edith, Dora and I went to Picture Palace[23] to hear the P[hilamonica] O[rchestra]. Very good.

Had a good day in spite of weather. It didn't half rain when I came home.

Monday 20 October - Having a try for the *Daily Mirror* £1000 [competition]; sent twenty coupons in. What would I be able to do if only I won.

Wednesday 22 October - Had a sleep in the afternoon. Went up to Edith's after tea. We had a walk over the hills. I was very happy indeed.

Thursday 23 October - Mended a puncture then had a cycle ride up as far as Marsden, the furthest I have been on a cycle for nine years. Had a puncture coming home, called at Edith's to mend it.

Saturday 25 October - Leeds Road with Herbert; an awful game, [Huddersfield] Town loose first match of the season. Edith and I tried to get into Hipperdrome but were unlucky, so went to Premier [cinema], then home. Had a bit of fun between getting there and coming home. I am ever so happy.

Monday 27 October - Met Edith in Milnsbridge, had an election meeting of our own (Figure 10). I'll bet she can't weigh my politics up. Had a bit of fun, Lewis was with me.

Wednesday 29 October - Election Day and a beastly one too; didn't go up to Edith's, had the night off.[24]

Thursday 30 October - Met Edith in Town at seven. Went to Picture House, a decent show. I lost my bet with her and now I owe her a fur coat; I may buy her one, some day.

Figure 10. Paddock and Milnsbridge. *Kirklees Cultural Services*

Friday 31 October - Again met Edith after Tec[hnical College]. I enjoy these meetings, I only have her for an hour, but it is an hour.

Saturday 1 November - A vile day. Never went out until teatime, then Edith and I went for Hilda's coal then back home. Four of us played table tennis, we did have a good time. Yes, I think I have won alright as I hardly think all the love is on one side, but it isn't wise to be too sure.

Sunday 2 November - More rain, therefore more rest. Went to Chapel in the evening and had the room to ourselves for an hour afterwards, need I say more?

Saturday 8 November - Ida, Edith, Jack and I went to Leeds. Had a right good old shop window rant. I bought Edith's birthday present, namely an umbrella. Had a good time, but weather might have been better.

Sunday 9 November - *Creation* at Baptist.[25] Hilda sings, and although she is full of cold, [she] does very well indeed; as I have said before, she can sing. Fred asks me to be his best man, I refer him to Jack.

Wednesday 12 November - Edith and I went to Netherton with Hilda. Had a fine time. I like to hear Hilda sing.

Saturday 15 November - Went to Northumberland Street[26] with Edith; Frank and his wife there. Hilda is again singing, had a fine concert. Walked home with Edith and Hilda. Had a real fine time.

Sunday 16 November - The triplets become twenty-five years [old]. Had a walk in the evening after Chapel, a lovely evening, typical for lovers.

Monday 17 November - Met Edith in Milnsbridge, had a walk round the market.

Tuesday 18 November - Again I see her after Tec[hnical College].

Wednesday 19 November - Went up to Edith's in the evening, didn't go out but I was happy all the same.

Friday 21 November - Once again I spend and hour with Edith, the best hour of the day.

Saturday 22 November - Leeds Road [Football Ground]. Edith's after tea. We had the house to ourselves after I had shaved her dad. Need I say any more, only I was very very happy.

Tuesday 25 November - Went to see Jack at work, very interesting. Edith has her tooth drawn, see her at nine.

Thursday 4 December - I visit the dentist and have three teeth drawn and decide to have all my top ones out.

Saturday 6 December - Went to watch [Huddersfield] Town play Sunderland and it was a fine day and a fine game.[27] Went to Pictures with Edith in the evening. Dear little Edith she is my life absolutely. I could not live without her.

Sunday 7 December - Had a walk after Chapel which was very enjoyable.

Monday 8 December - Had another seven teeth drawn, that finishes the top ones, thank goodness they are all out. I feel a bit queer, so go to bed early; I'll be alright tomorrow.

Tuesday 9 December - Edith not very pleased with me because I do perhaps a little too much running about for Hilda but [I] suppose my heart is soft and I can't help it.

Wednesday 10 December - Went to bed in the afternoon and then Edith and I went to Premier to hear the Hand Bell Ringers, which were very good.[28] I always feel very happy on a Wednesday.

Friday 12 December - Met Edith after school. Walked up home and then shaved her father ready for the big event.

Saturday 13 December - Fred Shaw gets married. Jack is best man, I am groomsman. Went to and from Batley by taxi. Had a real good day but the weather was beastly. That's one wedding. Presume Jack's will be the next, then I wonder how long my own will be? I don't care how soon it is.

Sunday 14 December - Baptist *Messiah*,[29] enjoyed that. Had a walk. Went up to Edith's after Chapel and had some music. I also enjoyed that.

Saturday 20 December - Went to Town to buy Edith a watch [for Christmas], then went by [tram]car to Almondbury and had a walk. I wanted her to have a watch and not a slave bangle.

Sunday 21 December - Went to Crosland Moor *Messiah* in the evening then had a walk. It was such a lovely evening I was ever so happy. It's great to be alive and to have a girl and to be loved.

Wednesday 24 December [Christmas Eve] - Jack, Ida and Edith came down home to supper then seven of us went to hear the bells. Had a great time. Jack and myself went to Lewis's after we had left our girls, and came rolling home about three after a grand time.

Thursday 25 December [Christmas Day] - Edward gets married. All the boys are there. I take a few photographs. Edith comes home to tea; a real nice time.

Friday 26 December [Bank Holiday] - Four of us go to Leeds Road [Football Ground]. After tea Edith and I stay in then have a little walk. I was ever so happy.

Sunday 28 December - Went to Herbert's to tea. Had a decent time. My people were also there.

Monday 29 December - Joined the Huddersfield Building Society.

Went to Milnsbridge and saw Edith. I could have stayed all night with her. I did not want to come home.

Wednesday 31 December - Had a sleep in the afternoon. Had a good evening. I was with Edith, so the old year goes out with a glad heart. I have seen twenty-five Christmas's but never have I spent one as happily as my last. Love has never been a part of my rejoicings, Edith I thank you for all you have done for me. I hope you always love me as now.

Notes and References

1. Grand Theatre, Manchester Road. David Powell in *The Mystery Road.*
2. Hipperdrome Theatre, Huddersfield. C E Williams and Charles Beanland present the pantomime *Little Red Riding Hood.*
3. Banisters, on Byram Street. They had a grocery shop at the front which made home deliveries on request and a waitress service cafe at the back up a few stairs.
4. 'Premier' Picture Palace Cinema, Paddock Head. Grace Davison and Montague Love in *Man's Plaything.*
5. Palace Theatre, Huddersfield. *Jack of All Trades,* advertised as 'a naval melodramusical affair.'
6. Picturedrome, Buxton Road. *Flames of Passion* featuring Mae Marsh. Billed as 'undoubtedly the finest picture ever shown in Huddersfield.'
7. Empire Picture House Theatre, Huddersfield. Mae Murray in *Fascination.* 'Gorgeous Gowns and Brilliant Dancing.'
8. Bull's Eyes, slang name for a policeman's flashlight or hand-held lamp, which had a thick glass lens over the light to magnify the light beam.
9. Longwood Sing, known in Huddersfield as the 'Mother of all sings'. Started in 1873 and takes place annually at Nab End Tower, Longwood, a folly erected in the nineteenth century to provide employment for local men out of work.
10. Princess Mary visited Huddersfield in connection with the opening of the new YMCA premises in John Street. HRH detrained at Bradley Station and was driven into Huddersfield. The *Huddersfield Daily Examiner* reported that the weather consisted of snow, sleet and rain, and that outdoor activities had to be curtailed due to the bad weather. Many started queuing in Huddersfield town centre from 11.30am for an afternoon arrival.
11. Palmist or fortune-teller.
12. Corporation Popular Concert and Organ Recital at the Huddersfield Town Hall. The *Huddersfield Daily Examiner* reported 'Miss Hilda Shaw displayed a good soprano voice with beautiful clear head-notes in Gounod's 'Far Greater in His Lowly State' and Sanderson's 'Be Still, Blackbird.'
13. Princess Picture House and cafe, Northumberland. Lillian and Dorothy Gish in D W Griffith's *Orphan's in the Snow.* 'Special return visit by request of numerous patrons.'
14. This I think is a misprint, and should read *Tuesday.*
15. Lime washing (sometimes known as distemper); a mixture of lime and water which is painted onto the walls of houses in place of wallpaper.
16. Almondbury 44 v Bradley Mills 80. J Wilkinson bowled Philips 0. As this is the only person on both sides with the initial J, it can be reasonably assumed that this is Jack who 'had to have his leg pulled' for being taken for a duck.
17. This obviously refers to the entry above which he penned under the wrong date; and the suggestion 'I must be in love' alludes to his confused state of mind which made him absent-mindedly write it here.
18. Lascelles Hall v Almondbury; rain stopped play.
19. Courage, tenacity
20. Almondbury Rush. An annual fair held in the village. Many villages held such events under various titles. I recall numerous visits to the 'Kirkheaton Rant' held in a field behind the public house adjacent to the church. We would walk to this fair from Bradley.
21. Cowcliffe Sing. A similar event to the Longwood Sing, but with a more religious bias.
22. Huddersfield Town Reserves 6 v Aston Villa Reserves 1.

23. This was possibly the Milnsbridge Picture Palace.

24. Series of local by-elections; Mr Enoch Hill, JP (Con) supported Stanley Baldwin and spoke at various places including Crosland Moor; Primrose Hill and Milnsbridge.

25. *The Creation,* oratorio by F J Hayden (1732-1809). Words from *Genesis* and *Paradise Lost* translated into German and re-translated into English. First performed Vienna, 1798; London, 1800.

26. This could be a mistake as the only major concert reported for that date was the Town Hall Popular Concert and Organ Recital at which Hilda Shaw sang the previous year.

27. Huddersfield Town 6 v Sunderland 0.

28. Premier Cinema, Paddock. Norma Talmadge in *The Sign on the Door.* During the intervals the Crosland Moor Public Handbell Ringers conducted by J Ellis performed.

29. *The Messiah,* oratorio by G F Handel (1685-1759). Liberetto selected from scriptures by Charles Jenner. Composed in just three weeks in 1741. First performed Dublin, 1742; London, 1743.

9. HUDDERSFIELD AND THE 'WIRELESS'

by John White

RADIO, OR 'THE WIRELESS', as it was known at the time was very popular in the early 1920s and 30s. It was an exciting new technology that could be easily accessed with the simplest of equipment, namely the 'cat's whisker' or simple crystal set. This type of set could easily be home-made from simple materials but listening was a solitary affair since the output could just about drive a pair of headphones, there being no amplification to drive a loudspeaker. The aerial used had to be long and preferably outdoors in order to pick up the strongest signal. Some of the more adventurous types even managed to build valve sets to give more sensitivity and enable loudspeakers to be used allowing all the family to listen in. Valve receivers however required a separate power supply and this normally took the form of batteries which had to be re-charged regularly, it was quite a common sight to see people taking their little glass 'accumulators' along to the local bicycle shop or ironmongers to get a 'top up'.

At first the broadcasters who provided the programmes were independent of each other and their output was very much experimental, large towns and cities were served by transmitters owned and run by big companies like Marconi or GEC. The transmitter at Manchester, callsign 2ZY, was run by the Metropolitan-Vickers company and being low powered probably struggled to reach much more than twenty miles radius. The Huddersfield area was therefore poorly served by radio at that time as far as local services were concerned but, due to the vagaries of the upper atmosphere, it would have been just possible to receive some of the high-powered continental stations after dark, albeit with some degree of fading and distortion.

The British Broadcasting Company was formed in 1922 after the government, under the guidance of the Post Office, decided that broadcasting should be put on a more organised footing. Thus the BBC at this time was made up of all the main commercial companies involved in the radio industry and its first Chief Engineer, in fact at one point its only one! was Captain Peter Eckersley, a colourful personality and talented performer as well as a clever technician. He originally worked for the Marconi Company and in addition to the engineering work on their transmitter, callsign 2MT - known as 'Two

Emma Tock', he also acted in plays and did some singing over the air! Eckersley was recruited by the formidable John Reith, later Sir John, the General Manager of the Company, a strict authoritarian with a definite view of how the BBC should develop as a public service organisation. Reith was the son of a Scottish minister and was trained as a mechanical engineer although his talents lay in the managerial and organisational fields.

The new BBC soon had a plan in place to provide transmitters up and down the country to serve large areas of population. One was set up in Leeds in July of 1924, callsign 2LS, and at the same time another was provided in Bradford to relay the programmes from Leeds. Eckersley was always aware that radio should not just be the prerogative of the technically minded few but should provide entertainment of a good quality and at sufficient signal strength. He also believed that a variety of programmes should be available to the listener. To this end he developed what was known as the 'Regional Scheme'. This involved the provision of high-powered stations at rural sites around the country but still within reach of main population centres. Each station would consist of two transmitters, one providing a National programme of general news and entertainment and the other giving a Regional programme to reflect the local characteristics of the area that it served. The first of these stations was built at Brookmans Park, fifteen miles north of London, and opened in 1928. The BBC by this time had been transformed into a 'Corporation' from the old 'Company' and was freed from commercial control into an independent body financed solely through the purchase of wireless licences bought by the listener. The regional scheme was now well developed and plans went ahead to find an appropriate site for the next station in the sequence. Also at this time Peter Eckersley was forced to leave the BBC due to his involvement in a divorce case but the parting was not unfriendly, it was a requirement of the rules of the Corporation and reflected the social conditions of the time. Eckersley retained an admiration and respect for Reith and his achievements throughout his life.

Moorside Edge takes shape
Following the opening of the London Regional Station at Brookmans Park steps were already being taken to find the best site for the new North Regional Station. A mobile transmitter and aerial system was used at suitably selected locations. From measurements of the received signal predictions could be made as to the expected signal strength in the towns and cities, allowing for the fact that the final

transmitted power would be much higher than that from a simple mobile unit. These tests took place in 1929 and from the results three possible sites were chosen, namely Barkisland, Sowerby Bridge and Moorside Edge at Pole Moor, near Slaithwaite. There was in Huddersfield at this time a thriving Radio Society whose members built their own sets and took a great deal of interest in the fact that Huddersfield was shortly to have its own transmitting station. Consequently the progress of the station's planning and construction was followed with great interest and these were faithfully reported in the local newspapers, the *Huddersfield Daily Examiner* and the *Colne Valley Guardian* in particular. As an indication of the interest that radio generated at the time, both newspapers had their own weekly technical column, variously known as 'Wireless Jottings' or 'Wireless Notes', and written by 'Radio Jax' in the *Examiner* or 'Wireless Hints and Tips' by 'Rados' in the *Guardian*. Great interest was further aroused when it was announced that no less a person than Eckersley himself would visit Huddersfield in November of 1928 and it was hoped that some clues as to the site of the new station or indeed an official announcement would be made during the visit. The meeting took place in the Town Hall on 10 November and was attended by a variety of civic dignatories including the Lord Mayor and members of the Council together with members of the Huddersfield Engineering Society, the Huddersfield Radio Society and representatives of the local radio retail trade, including some from Manchester. Eckersley however only spoke on 'the future of broadcasting' in general terms and answered questions at the end but kept a discrete silence on the new transmitter, electing only to say that the provision of a new station was a complex thing and that an announcement would be made on the North Regional station at the 'appropriate time'.

It became something of a detective story from then on as far as the site of the new station was concerned, with people picking up clues from various sources and drawing their own conclusions. In September 1929 it was noted that the Post Office had laid a new cable to Pickletop Lane, near Moorside Edge, and later that same month a new cable was laid through Huddersfield town centre, this had 200 pairs with eight being 'specifically allocated for broadcasting'. Earlier, the Estate Agents Edgar England were appointed to arrange a three month option-of-purchase on the land in July and so, with all the activity on the site, it was an open secret that Moorside Edge would indeed be the place. Even so, the BBC maintained a strict policy of 'no comment' on the decision and this caused much annoyance and frustration among the local radio fraternity. One gentleman expressed this by writing to 'Radio Jax' complaining that because of the delay he could not plan his winter constructing activities, the expected high signal strength of the new station would probably swamp out his sensitive receiver should he decide to build one. Indeed this problem of distant stations being drowned out by a much more powerful station right on the doorstep was one that concerned many people. At that time many listeners enjoyed picking up the strong continental stations which broadcast popular music and dance tunes of the day and local newspapers regularly printed details of programmes from European stations. The BBC, under John Reith, tended to restrict this style of programming and on Sundays it was kept off the air completely as a mark of respect to the Sabbath. Receivers at that time were not selective enough to discriminate between strong signals close together in wavelength terms and the stronger stations tended to spread widely over the dial so listeners were understandably concerned that the new transmitter would block out some of their favourite foreign stations.

Moorside Edge is Built
At last, the official announcement that the 'North Regional Station of the BBC would be built at Moorside Edge, near Huddersfield' was made in early October 1929 in the journal *World Radio*, a companion publication to Radio Times. Construction work began almost immediately with improvements to approach roads and preliminary work on foundations. The work continued throughout the winter with the weather, as always, providing its own problems. The work progressed well however and the main building began to take shape and provide a noticeable landmark on the skyline as the months passed. The sight of this new wonder of technology, and in particular the masts, attracted great interest and it was common for people of the surrounding area, and further afield, to be drawn to them and follow the progress of their construction. The noted technical journal *Wireless World* reported that 'the inhabitants of Slaithwaite now spend their evenings in trips to Moorside Edge to observe the progress at the North Regional', it was regularly reported that crowds of people used to gather near the site making it almost a regular outing for some families. The *Colne Valley Guardian* reported that by June 1930 'excellent progress had been made' and 'from Manchester Road it may be seen that the building is taking a well defined shape on the sky line, and already the inhabitants of Slaithwaite are pointing it out with a sense of pride and proprietorship to their visitors from other districts'.

The three masts, when completed, were each 500 feet high and this was one of the first radio stations to have such tall structures. Brookmans Park was restricted in the height of its masts due to Air Ministry requirements and so it had smaller self-supporting towers as opposed to the guyed masts at Moorside Edge. In order for them to endure the rigours of the weather, especially the strong winds, it was necessary that they be allowed to move, consequently each sat on a steel ball at the base allowing them to sway out of the vertical during very strong gales. The masts supported the wire aerials which were slung between them with the Regional programme using a T-shaped aerial and the National programme using a vertical wire. Mention has been made previously of the weather and even in summer it could change very rapidly with mist, rain and wind being common problems. An Irish workman - who else?- was quoted as saying, in September, 'och nivver did I see such a place as this. If it isn't fog its rain, and if it isn't rain its wind. Nivver hardly is there a chance to work.' The *Examiner's* reporter noted that on the day of his visit the mast was 'bent over like a bow, the top being 10 feet out of the perpendicular'.

These regular progress reports were given in the local newspapers and reporters who turned up at the site were greeted with a mixture of receptions, one said 'it was easier for a rich man to enter into Heaven than to drag information from the officials at Moorside Edge'. However another visit a few weeks later resulted in the reporter being 'most courteously received' and given an impromptu guided tour but warned not to be too inquisitive and not to take any photographs inside the building.

Moorside Calling!
Finally, with the building and masts completed in December of 1930, the technical equipment was installed and preliminary testing began in March of 1931. This was the time all keen listeners in the area were waiting for and they eagerly tuned their receivers waiting for the first signals. The *Examiner* reported the first transmissions being broadcast in late February although the official BBC test programmes were not announced until March. It was reported that the first words heard were 'we regret that owing to a technical hitch..!' Comments were initially favourable and one of Huddersfields' main radio retailers, Taylors of Lord Street, took the opportunity to check the degree of swamping over the wavebands from the strong signals. Twelve receivers were used and it was reported that all exhibited spreading over the bands, with the shortwave band being totally swamped. The best of them showed a twenty per cent swamping over the dial.

The name of the station caused quite a bit of controversy, and jealousy! among the people of Huddersfield and Slaithwaite. Both camps thought that their town's name should be included in the official title. Some thought that 'Huddersfield Calling' should be the name, others commented that 'Moorside Edge it cannot be since that is a coined word and represents nothing but a stretch of half moorland country'. If the BBC insisted on the 'North Regional transmitter' then Brookmans Park should be called the 'South Regional transmitter'. The good folk of Slaithwaite had a council meeting on the subject and 'Slaithwaite Calling' was suggested but, following representations to the BBC, the Corporation responded that the official name would be the 'North Regional' and when necessary the geographical position would be known as 'Slaithwaite, near Huddersfield' which presumably placated both camps. Some people had suspicions that they had originally left out 'Slaithwaite' because nobody in the BBC could pronounce it properly!

In April the BBC's Head of North Region, Mr G D Liveing, and the Engineer-in-Charge, Mr E F Wheeler, arranged a reception for a number of representatives of the press. Speeches were made and Mr Liveing revealed that the BBC had received several applications for the posts of Announcer and Musical Director at Moorside Edge! Some writers had expressed sympathy with the programme staff now that they had to move from their comfortable studios in Manchester and Leeds to a 'bleak and desolate spot' like Moorside Edge! However he did reassure them that the BBC would not be setting up a 'bungalow colony at Pole Moor' and no one would have to move!

A very good account of the visit was published in the Examiner in which the reporter described 'the wonders of Moorside Edge' and the equipment as being like something from science fiction with 'twinkling bulbs of green and red, and dials with their nervous flickering fingers. It has the appearance of a film set designed for some elaborate glimpse into the future'. Another comment stated

> at the control desk there sits an engineer - I almost said a robot for it certainly seems he is the servant and not the master of the amazing apparatus.

The Yorkshire Observer's reporter called it 'a radio house of wonder'.

Another visit for members of Slaithwaite council and their wives took place in May. Everyone was most impressed with the facilities and the wife of one councillor noted how clean everything was, particularly the engine room, 'it would shame some human living rooms' she remarked. She then quoted an overheard comment from one councillor to his wife 'could you beat this, mother?'

The National programme officially started on 12 May 1931 and the Regional programme followed shortly on the 2 July.

Technically the station followed much the same design as the first regional at Brookmans Park with the exception of the masts as previously mentioned. The two Marconi transmitters each had a power of 50kw and consisted of five separate units and a control desk (Figure 1). The station was virtually self-contained in that it had four large diesel-driven generators to provide its power and there was a 200,000 gallon reservoir for water supplies used for cooling the high power transmitting valves and also cooling the engines (Figure 2). The provision of the reservoir was prompted by the occurence of a drought in the area some years previously.

The building itself measured 300 feet by 120 feet at its widest point

Figure 1. Main transmitter hall showing one transmitter and control desk

Figure 2. The author in the engine room at Moorside Edge, 1974

Figure 3. View of Moorside Edge in 1980 showing one mast partially dismantled prior to moving to a new position.

and was designed to reflect the importance of broadcasting in the life of the country at that time (Figures 3 and 4). Eckersley commented that these buildings should have a motto above the door to the effect that 'it is better to transmit than to receive' but the suggestion was never taken up! Since the height above sea level was just over 1000 feet it had to withstand severe winter weather conditions and the aerial system could be prone to icing up. This could cause problems for the transmitters as well as increasing the loading strain on the masts. In order to combat this effect two 'de-icing' machines were installed. These were large generators which could be connected to the aerial system after closedown and pass a current of hundreds of amperes through the feeders, keeping the ice at bay. Also, after closedown the engines were stopped and the load transferred to a large storage battery of 2000 Ampere/hour capacity. To prevent vibrations from the

Figure 4. The front of the main building in 1975

diesel engines reaching the sensitive programme circuits, the engines themselves sat on a huge 600 ton concrete raft which, in turn, sat on a layer of cork-like material. This whole area was then separated from the main foundations by a three inch air gap bridged over by teak boards flush with the floor.

A small studio was provided for emergency purposes equipped with a microphone and twin turntable record desk together with a collection of 78 rpm records. These were mostly classical, it was not certain whether they included the famous 'Teddy Bear's Picnic' - a favourite test record among studio engineers!

Later History

The period from 1931 - 1939 passed uneventfully for the station, there was talk of testing the programme lines for the suitability of television transmissions using the thirty-line Baird system. Brookmans Park had been used to test the system in the London area, using one transmitter for vision and the other for sound. No reports were found of this taking place at Moorside Edge but its unlikely as the pictures produced were very crude and soon the superior EMI all-electronic system would win the day, but that's another story!

With the advent of war in 1939 both National and Regional programme services were ended and one 'Home Service' created, followed in 1940 by the 'Forces Programme'. Considerable technical changes took place over the period of the war, connection to the public electricity supply and extra transmitters being installed. The building was extended and changes to the frequencies were necessary to enable broadcasting to the occupied countries of Europe. The domestic transmitters were incorporated into 'synchronised groups' along with other sites to prevent them being used as homing beacons by the Luftwaffe. Each transmitter used the same frequency and if one was switched off - which RAF Fighter Command could order at a moments notice - the service would still be heard by listeners from the other stations in the group but at a reduced signal strength. One of the transmitters was even used to jam German fighter communications and modified to allow quick changes of frequency to follow any attempts by the enemy to switch to a clear channel.

In 1944 the American forces set up a network called ABSIE, the American Broadcasting Service in Europe, to provide news and comment to Europe in preparation for the coming invasion and beyond. A building was provided at the side of the Rochdale road, near to the present Jack'o'Mitre pub and two RCA 50kw transmitters were installed together with suitable aerials. This building actually existed until the 1980s, mainly used as a cow shed! traces of it can still be seen although the present owners have amended and extended it. Later, one of the transmitters was installed in the main building in the 1950s and used for the Light Programme. These transmitters proved useful in the severe winter of 1947 when the main aerial system was damaged and they were put back into use. The mains electricity supply then failed and the station was forced to use the diesel generators continuously. With only a few days fuel remaining, staff had to man-handle oil drums across the fields to replenish the supply, the weather making the roads impassable.

In the 1950s early experiments in the new FM transmission system were done at Moorside Edge and one of the first mobile maintenance teams in the BBC was based there to cope with the increased use of small, low powered, unattended radio transmitters.

In the 1960s pirate radio forced the BBC to provide a new 'pop' service and Radio One was started in 1967. The Light programme transmitter was used for this service and the Light programme itself transferred to the Droitwich long wave transmitting station near Birmingham. The decisions of an international conference meant a great upheaval in changes to frequencies for all BBC medium wave transmitters in 1978 and consequently Moorside Edge lost its Radio Four service and gained Radio Two and Radio Three, Radio One transferring to a higher powered transmitter. The three old masts were demolished and two new ones provided, wire aerials were used for Radios One and Three, Radio Two used the masts themselves as aerials.

Fall and Rise

By the 1980s the station had been in existence for over fifty years and the original engines and transmitters were still in use. A programme of re-engineering was proposed for all BBC regional stations with new, more efficient transmitters and improved programme and moni-toring equipment, enabling the station to operate with no staff in attendance. Brookmans Park and Droitwich were the first stations to be modernised but the process of installing new equipment in existing old buildings proved unsatisfactory and it was decided that a completely new building should be built at Moorside Edge. This took place between 1983 and 1986, the old building was then closed and the equipment scrapped. Some items went to local museums and collectors, finally the building was demolished and the site landscaped and returned to the local farmer for grazing.

Figure 5. View of Moorside Edge across the Colne Valley, 1974. *(Examiner)*

The Present Day

Today at Moorside Edge there stands a low-profile, industrial-style building similar to many such structures covering the landscape these days, only the two 500 feet high masts betray its true purpose. The BBC no longer owns the site or the station, all its transmitters were sold off to an American/French consortium in 1996 and the money used to finance the next revolution in broadcasting - digital. The only BBC programme radiated from Moorside Edge now is Radio Five Live, the Radio One and Radio Three frequencies were surrendered to the commercial operators Talk Radio and Virgin Radio following the Conservative government's ruling that there should be no dupli-cation of programmes on Medium wave and VHF-FM. New, all solid-state, transmitters were installed for the commercial operators and satellite programme feeds were used.

Thus Moorside Edge continues its existence through times of great technological change, vastly altered from its original state and probably unnoticed by the majority of people who pass by. After all, there are so many masts these days; television stations, mobile radio stations and mobile 'phone sites all crowd the horizon competing for space on the hillsides as well as in the ether. Who knows, maybe one day some passing traveller may stop and gaze at the hills above Slaithwaite one dark evening and see the faint ghostly shape of a third mast and a brightly lit building on the sky-line and, if he listens carefully, and with some imagination, he may even hear the faint strains of the 'Teddy Bear's Picnic' and the announcer say 'Huddersfield Calling!' - now there's a thought!

Acknowledgements and Notes

The author gratefully acknowledges help from the following sources:
The staff and facilities of Huddersfield Central Library.
The staff and facilities of Bradford Central Library.
The staff and facilities of Halifax Central Library.
The *Huddersfield Examine* for one photograph
All other photographs were taken by the author.

Sources

The Huddersfield Daily Examiner
The Huddersfield Weekly Examiner
The Colne Valley Guardian
The Yorkshire Observer
Wireless World
BBC Yearbooks 1928 - 1947
Eckersley PP, *The Power Behind the Microphone*, Jonathan Cape 1941
Pawley E, *BBC Engineering 1922 -1972*, BBC Publications 1972

CONTRIBUTORS

1. COINS TOKENS AND MEDALS OF THE HUDDERSFIELD DISTRICT

John Rumsby is a Londoner by birth, but has lived in Yorkshire for over twenty years. After taking a degree in Archaeology and Geography at the University of Southampton, his first job was in a regimental museum in Durham. He is now Museum Collections Manager for Kirklees Council's Community History Service. John's interest in numismatics started with his discovery of a drawer of coins and tokens in Hull Museums rescued many years before from the ruins of the City Museum's original building, bombed during the Second World War. The task of sorting and identifying these coins introduced him to the important contribution such material can make to local history. He has published a number of articles and other works on museum collections, numismatics and military history.

2. THE MANOR OF HONLEY AT WORK 1784-1881

John Goodchild is a native of Wakefield and was educated at the Grammar school there. He has been active in local history research since about the age of thirteen, and is the author of 140 books and published essays on aspects of the history of the West Riding. He was founder-Curator of Cusworth Hall Museum and subsequently Archivist to Wakefield MDC; in his retirement he runs a unique Local History Study Centre at Wakefield which houses his immense collection of manuscripts and research material which is open to use, free of charge, by appointment. Mr Goodchild holds an honorary M Univ from the Open University, awarded for academic and scholarly distinction and for public services. Outside historical research, his interests lie in Freemasonry and in Unitarianism - and his dog.

3. THE WHOLE HOG: HUDDERSFIELD CHARTISM 1838-1855

Alan Brooke, a former miner at Emley Moor Colliery, studied Archaeology and Ancient History at Manchester University. He has written several pamphlets and articles on the working class history of the Huddersfield area, including *Liberty or Death*, co-authored with Lesley Kipling, an account of early nineteenth century Luddism and Radicalism. As a founder member of the Socialist Labour Party in West Yorkshire, he claims some insight into the problems that confronted local Chartists! He is currently working on an illustrated record of the textile mills of Huddersfield and Vicinity c.1790-1914.

4. SUSAN SUNDERLAND THE 'YORKSHIRE QUEEN OF SONG'

John A Hargreaves was a founder member and former Vice-Chairman of the Huddersfield Local History Society and taught for nearly twenty years at King James's School, Almondbury, where he was Head of History and Religious Education. A native of Burnley and a graduate of Southampton University, he subsequently obtained MA and PhD degrees at Huddersfield University through part-time study. He is currently Head of Humanities at Howden Clough Girls' High School, Batley and honorary secretary and editor of the Halifax Antiquarian Society. He has lectured and written extensively on local history, contributed to radio and television documentaries and twice been awarded the Yorkshire History Prize. His publications include books on Halifax and Sowerby Bridge, articles for *Northern History* and the *New Dictionary of National Biography* and chapters in *Huddersfield: a most handsome town* (1992) and *The Representation and Reality of War* (1999) He is married with four children and lives in Halifax.

5. LEGENDS OF THE COLNE VALLEY

John A Oldham lives in the Colne Valley. He was born in Bradford and is married to Elaine, a schoolteacher. They have two children, Andrew and Amelia. Educated at Buttershaw Comprehensive School, he studied printing at Leeds College of Technology and management at Leeds Polytechnic. Joined Waddingtons, the 'Monopoly' and Playing Card Manufactures in Leeds, as a management trainee. After a spell with Yorkshire Television became Production Director of a Publishing Company, specialising in educational materials and short run reprint books.

Subsequently appointed General Manager of Regent Print Ltd that was closed in the early 1980s recession. He bought the goodwill of his old company with his redundancy money and it is still in business today. He is an advisor for the Prince' s Youth Business Trust and has written a history of Golcar for young people and a guided walk around the village.

6. BRUCE OF HUDDERSFIELD

Isobel Margaret Schofield trained at the College of Librarianship, Wales at Aberystyth. Born in Huddersfield she has been associated with Highfield Congregationl Church since the age of eleven and a member of Highfield St James since the two churches united in 1978. A member of the choir she is Church archivist and a member of the Group magazine editorial team. Her work as Publications Librarian for Kirklees Libraries has involved her in the publication of many books including *Huddersfield: a Most Handsome Town* and more recently two joint publications with Breedon Books and the Huddersfield Examiner, *Images of Huddersfield* and *The Heritage of Huddersfield*. Other publications include a booklet entitiled Mirfield and a leaflet on Almondbury. She is married with one son.

7. EARLY DAYS IN THE MILL

Fred Wood was born above a butcher's shop in Shore Head in Huddersfield in 1913. The family later settled in Holmfirth moving to Burnlee where he educated. Fed was partially blinded by ulcers as a child and has suffered from rheumatism all his life. In spite of his illness he has spent over 50 years in the textile industry and has spent part of his retirement writing about his early days in textile mills, of which this essay is just a small part.

8. THE DIARY OF AN UNKNOWN

Alan Whitworth trained at Bradford College of Art, a past member of the Yorkshire & Humberside Federation of Museums & Art Galleries and an Associate Member of the Tourism Society, from 1977, after a number of years in the world of printing and graphic design, Alan Whitworth predominately turned his attention to promoting the preservation of English parish churches, founding and running a charity to that end (SPEC), writing and lecturing on the subject, mounting many exhibitions and organising the first national conference dealing with churches and tourism - yet his interests are wider, and his regards for old buildings have led in one area after a study of dovecotes and pigeon lofts about which he has written and lectured often, to the founding of the Yorkshire Dovecote Society, of which he his secretary, and in another, to compile a number of records about places with which he has been associated.

Alan Whitworth is a member of the Monumental Brass Society and founder of the Whitworth One-Name Study Group; he is also a trustee of the North Yorkshire Moors Buildings Preservation Trust. Married, he lectures part-time at Bradford University on architectural and local history subjects. Alan Whitworth is the author of many articles and several books including *Exploring Churches* (1986); *Dorset Dovecotes* (1988); *Whitby As They Saw It* (1991); *Yorkshire Windmills* (1991); *Village Tales - The Story of Scalby* (1993) and four titles in the 'Times Pasts series - *Bradley* (1986); *Thornton* (1987); *Bradford* (1987) and *Weymouth* (1989). He has also compiled two bibliographies on Dovecotes and Pigeon Lofts.

9. HUDDERSFIELD AND THE 'WIRELESS'

John White was born in Glasgow. He joined the BBC in 1962 as a Technical Assistant. His first posting was to Penrith, Cumbria to the short-wave transmitting station at Skelton. In 1967 he moved to Huddersfield to take up an engineer post at Moorside Edge. He became a Senior Maintenance Engineer in 1975 and apart from short spells in Television at Pontop Pike, near Newcastle, and a period in London in the Technical Investigations Department, his main base was Huddersfield. In 1990, following the re-engineering and de-staffing of Moorside Edge, he was transferred to the Holme Moss transmitting station where he stayed until taking early retirement in 1995. He now works part-time for the *Huddersfield Daily Examiner.* Apart from radio and electronics his main hobbies are computing, photography and music. He has been known to strum the 'odd chord' in the St Patrick's Music Group!

INDEX

PEOPLE

PLACES

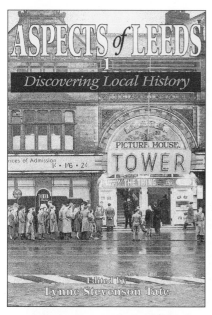

ASPECTS OF LEEDS 1
Discovering Local History
Edited by Lynne Stevenson Tate

ISBN: 1-871647-38-X – £9.95

ASPECTS LEEDS 2
Discovering Local History
Edited by Lynne Stevenson Tate

ISBN: 1-871647-59-2 – £9.95

50yrs STAGE AND SCREEN
by Arthur Riley

ISBN: 1-871647-69-X – £7.99

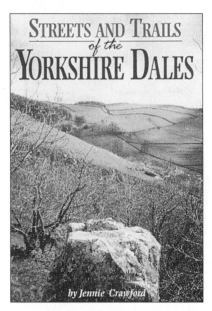

STREETS & TRAILS OF THE YORKSHIRE DALES
by Jennie Crawford

ISBN: 1-871647-72-X – £7.95

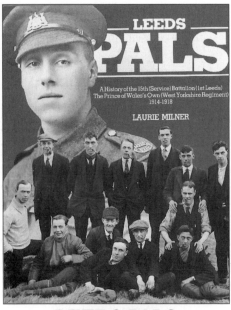

LEEDS PALS
by Laurie Milner

ISBN: 0-85052-634-5 – £17.95

FAILED TO RETURN
by Bill Norman

ISBN: 0-885052-474-1 – £17.95